faithful practices

faithful practices
everyday ways to feed your spirit

Erik Walker Wikstrom, Editor

Skinner House Books
Boston

www.skinnerhouse.org

Printed in the United States

Cover design by Kathryn Sky-Peck
Text design by Suzanne Morgan

print ISBN: 978-1-55896-811-0
eBook ISBN: 978-1-55896-812-7

6 5 4 3 2 1
19 18 17

Library of Congress Cataloging-in-Publication Data

Names: Wikstrom, Erik Walker, editor.
Title: Faithful practices : everyday ways to feed your spirit / Erik Walker Wikstrom, editor.
Description: Boston : Skinner House Books, 2017. | Includes bibliographical references.
Identifiers: LCCN 2017033584 (print) | LCCN 2017039130 (ebook) | ISBN
  9781558968127 | ISBN 9781558968110 (pbk. : alk. paper)
Subjects: LCSH: Spiritual life. | Spiritual life--Unitarian Universalist Association.
Classification: LCC BL624 (ebook) | LCC BL624.F355 2017 (print) | DDC 204/.4—dc23
LC record available at https://lccn.loc.gov/2017033584

"Alchemy of Love" from *The Love Poems of Rumi* by Deepak Chopra, copyright © 1998 by Deepak Chopra, M.D., used by permission of Harmony Books, an imprint of the Crown Publishing Group, a division of Penguin Random House LLC, all rights reserved, any third party use of this material, outside of this publication, is prohibited, interested parties must apply directly to Penguin Random House LLC for permission. The Scripture quotations contained herein are from the *New Revised Standard Version Bible*, copyright © 1989 by the Division of Christian Education of the National Council of the Churches of Christ in the U.S.A., and are used by permission, all rights reserved. Excerpt from "The Vacation," copyright © 2012 by Wendell Berry, reprinted by permission of Counterpoint Press.

An earlier version of "Finding a Teacher" by Wayne Arnason appeared in *Everyday Spiritual Practice: Simple Pathways for Enriching Your Life*, edited by Scott W. Alexander (Skinner House, 1999).

contents

practices born in daily life

introduction

If you are holding this book in your hands, you are likely interested in, or actively seeking, a deeper connection to that sacred something known by so many names yet by no name fully known—God, Eternal Presence, Spirit of Life, All in All, Love. Throughout our history, we humans have discovered and developed a wide variety of tools to aid us in our quest for this connection. These tools are generally referred to as spiritual practices.

Yet if you are holding *this* book in your hands, it is also likely that you've already at least partially surveyed the religious landscape and come up wanting. There is a vast array of books about prayer, meditation, contemplative reading, fasting, journaling, and any number of other traditional practices. Faith communities of all kinds offer classes and retreats, and there are online opportunities to study one of the "classic" techniques for discovering or deepening that connection. But you've picked up this book, and that suggests that you're quite likely searching for . . . something else.

You've come to the right place. *Faithful Practices* is not another anthology covering well-trod paths toward the sacred. Even when some of the contributors here *do* write about a recognizably "spiritual" practice, they do so from some unexpected perspectives. You will not find here recommendations for fitting yourself into some predetermined pattern. Instead, these pages offer an invitation to look at the ways your own life and living might *already* be presenting you opportunities to tune in more deeply to the sacred something, the call of which you may already be hearing, however faintly.

Before talking about any particular spiritual practices, however, we would be wise first to try to understand what we mean by the words. There are, of course, many definitions, many technical terms we can turn to in an attempt to quantify the ineffable. My own favorite response draws on the writings of the Unitarian Henry David Thoreau. In his classic book, *Walden*, he wrote about the reason he engaged with his experiment of living in a ten-foot-by-fifteen-foot single-room cabin at the edge of Walden Pond:

> I went to the woods because I wished to live deliberately, to front only the essential facts of life, and see if I could not learn what it had to teach, and not, when I came to die, discover that I had not lived. I did not wish to live what was not life, living is so dear; nor did I wish to practise resignation, unless it was quite necessary. I wanted to live deep and suck out all the marrow of life.

"I did not wish to live what was not life . . . ." In that simple phrase, Thoreau asserts that there are essentially two ways of living: One is a life lived truly, fully, vividly alive, while the other might be called mere existence. Perhaps not surprisingly, he thought that most people of his day were living "not-life." (After all, this is the man who wrote, "The mass of [humanity] lead lives of quiet desperation.")

Life and not-life. The observation of this dichotomy does not belong to Thoreau alone. The Buddhist traditions use the terms *delusion* and *enlightenment*: living as if asleep and living fully awake. The Christian traditions talk about living alive in the spirit and living dead in sin. Over and over, throughout the religious and spiritual traditions that humans have developed, we find the teaching that there are two ways of living in this world—in a way that is truly alive, and in a way that is not really alive.

We can define spirituality, then, as the quest to move from not-life to life, from being asleep to waking up, from death to life. Spiritual practice grows out of the awareness that this transition is not easy and that, once achieved, takes reinforcement. Jesus is said to have prayed regularly. Gautama Buddha is said to have meditated daily despite having achieved enlightenment.

There is a helpful analogy in the life of Pau Casals i Defilló, better known in the United States as Pablo Casals. He practiced scales every single day of his life even after he was generally regarded as the greatest cellist in history. He had practiced them on the day he died, at the age of ninety-six. When asked a few years earlier why such a master would continue to practice something as rudimentary as scales, he replied that he thought he was beginning to make some progress.

The spiritual quest is in many ways like the artistic quest. You could probably make some pleasing sounds if you picked up an instrument every once in a while, or create a painting that is pleasant to look at if you brought out your paints and brushes from time to time. You might even create something remarkable, but it would more than likely be a lucky surprise. If you want to really make progress, you need to practice. Often. Regularly. It takes some discipline. There is a reason that spiritual practice is often called *spiritual discipline*.

Yet spiritual disciplines don't have to be esoteric and ancient to be effective. In 1999, Skinner House Books, an imprint of the Unitarian Universalist Association, published *Everyday Spiritual Practice: Simple Pathways for Enrich-*

ing Your Life. It includes thirty-eight essays that Unitarian Universalist clergy and lay leaders wrote, each describing a spiritual practice that they have found particularly meaningful. These range from things you might expect—prayer and sacred reading, for instance—to perhaps less conventional practices such as parenting, recycling, and antiracism work. In many ways, that book, edited by Scott W. Alexander, laid the foundation for this anthology.

In the movie *My Dinner with Andre,* Andre Gregory and Wallace Shawn have an extended, wide-ranging conversation, covering everything from experimental theater to enlightenment. At one point, Shawn remarks,

> Tell me, why do we require a trip to Mount Everest in order to be able to perceive one moment of reality? I mean . . . I mean, is Mount Everest more "real" than New York? I mean, isn't New York "real"? I mean, you see, I think if you could become fully aware of what existed in the cigar store next door to this restaurant, I think it would just blow your brains out! I mean . . . I mean, isn't there just as much "reality" to be perceived in the cigar store as there is on Mount Everest?

Perhaps this is what Ralph Waldo Emerson, Thoreau's contemporary, had in mind when he said about miracles: "But the very word Miracle, as pronounced by Christian churches, gives a false impression; it is Monster. It is not one with the blowing clover and the falling rain."

We seem to be conditioned to see some things—miracles, for instance, or spirituality itself—as somehow separate from our normal, everyday life. Yet as the Vietnamese Buddhist monk and peace activist Thich Nhat Hanh writes in *Buddha Mind, Buddha Body,* "The miracle is not to walk on water or in thin air, but the miracle is to walk on the Earth." The same is true of spiritual practices—they can be acts as common-place as washing the dishes or sitting down to dinner with your loved ones. Nothing esoteric at all.

In fact, as noted earlier, you may not need to *add* a spiritual practice into your daily life. You may already be doing something that could suffice! Remember, though, that if the purpose of spirituality is to help you to live an awake, truly alive life, then you must approach your spiritual practice in an awake and truly alive way. If you wash your dishes, for instance, totally mindlessly, hardly aware of what you're doing because you're thinking about the events of the past day or the day to come, then the task really won't do much to move you into a more alive life. If, however, you use your dishwashing, or whatever else you might be doing, as a tool, a vehicle, leading you toward a more aware way of being, it can authentically be called a spiritual practice. Not everything we do is a spiritual practice, yet almost anything we do can be a spiritual practice, something that moves us toward more spiritual living. It is my hope, and the hope of all the contributing authors, that you will find in these pages something to help you on that journey.

Each person who has written a chapter is actively using the practice that they describe. Some of the authors are ordained ministers, some are laypeople. (Ordination does not grant one exclusive access to all things spiritual, and each of us can discover our own path to take us toward living life "that is life.") All of the contributors are Unitarian Universalists —a liberal religious movement with deep roots. Unitarian Universalists do not come together around shared creeds but, rather, a shared commitment to a vision of Beloved Community. On any given Sunday, you might find in one of our congregations Christians sitting next to Buddhists, atheists next to Muslims, and seekers next to Sikhs. What holds us together is our covenant to work together, despite our differences, toward the realization of our common vision.

You don't need to be a Unitarian Universalist to find benefit in these pages, however. In keeping with the intentional inclusiveness of our movement, there are no creedal barriers built into any of these practices. Whatever you believe—or don't believe—these practices can offer you a path. After all, the historic Buddha is remembered as saying that the world's many oceans have different names yet all have one taste (salty). Similarly, teachings have different names and different forms yet all "taste" like freedom. "Freedom" and "bondage" are other ways of describing life and not-life.

In other writing I have described what I call the Eight Spheres of Spiritual Practice. Drawing on a model for Zen training developed at Zen Mountain Monastery on Mount Tremper in New York, these eight spheres are like the U.S. Food and Drug Administration's "food pyramid." While neither is a perfect model, the intent is the same—there are different kinds of spiritual practices, just as there are different kinds of nutrient groups. It may be tempting to do only one kind of practice—just as it might be tempting to eat only carbohydrates—yet too much of any one thing is ultimately unhealthy. This doesn't mean that you have to have all eight kinds of practices going on in your life simultaneously, any more than you should have every kind of "food group" on your plate at every meal. In fact, you probably shouldn't. Over time, though, if your goal is to live a full and well-rounded spiritual life, it will be important to engage with each of these eight types of practices:

◆ Personal practices—that we do on our own
◆ Communal practices—that we do with others, in groups
◆ Partnership practices—that we do with one other person
◆ Mind practices—that engage our minds and our thinking

- Body practices—that get our physical selves involved
- Soul practices—that make use of our imagination and creativity
- Family practices—that are found in and around the people with whom we live and interact
- Justice practices—that engage us in the work of helping to heal this all-too-broken world

Some might say that this is too complex a model. They may point instead to only two kinds of spiritual practices—interior practices that draw you inward and exterior practices that bring you back out into the world. No matter how simple or complex the schema, though, the fundamental idea is the same: Our spiritual lives ought not to be monolithic. One practice, or one *kind* of practice, on its own, cannot fully engage all of you. Focusing only on the mind leaves out the body; focusing only on inner contemplation leaves out working for justice.

It is also important to avoid limiting our thinking to those things that "look" like a spiritual practice. The contributors to this book are not concerned with whether anyone else would recognize what they do as a spiritual practice; they are concerned only with whether what they do supports them in learning to be truly, fully, vividly alive. That's why there are chapters on everything from contemplative walking to making art to prayer to roller derby. And since the purpose of this book is to help *you* discover or develop a practice that helps *you* to live more truly, fully, and vividly alive, at the end of each chapter there are questions designed to encourage you to think about how you might adapt the practice you've just read about (or something like it) to your own life's circumstances.

Faithful Practices is organized around three categories:

- Practices Born in Tradition are practices that you might recognize as "traditional," such as praying, tending an altar, or going on a spiritual retreat. Yet the eight contributors to this section are not bound by the ways things have always been done, They bring a fresh sensibility to the way they engage with these practices. One, Jon Cleland Host's chapter on the Cosmala, presents a new interpretation of a prayer-bead practices as old as the Rosary and the Mala.

♦ Practices Born in Play may surprise you. From blowing bubbles to using your phone as a spiritual tool to roller derby to collecting and playing with action figures, these contributors have not only expanded the idea of what can be considered spiritual, they have stepped out of the box completely and left it behind.

♦ Practices Born in Life are, as the title suggests, everyday activities you may already do—taking a walk, chopping vegetables, or nurturing your friendships. Each of the seven contributors to this section, though, agree that what transforms these daily routines into spiritual practices is the addition of the awareness of them pointing to something larger than the activity itself.

If you are seeking a way to deepen your life, to learn to live in such a way, to paraphrase Thoreau, as not to look back at your life and discover that you had not really lived, the practices explored in this book may present a path for you. If you already have a practice, even one of the practices described in this book, the varied approaches and understandings of these authors may expand your own experiences. In any case, drink deep, and "suck the marrow" out of the possibilities.

—Erik Walker Wikstrom

practices born in tradition

learning to pray

sue magidson

I used to think that a spiritual practice was something you did. Regularly. Pretty much the same way each time. Then, fifteen years ago, I began a daily prayer practice. Which keeps transforming itself. And continues to this day. And has changed my life.

If you'd told me fifteen years ago that prayer would be at the heart of my spiritual practice, I would have rolled my eyes and politely suggested that perhaps you'd confused me with someone else. As a lifelong Jewish Unitarian Universalist who grew up in a (then) atheistic UU congregation, prayer made me squirm. Public prayer offended me on ethical grounds—theists foisting their beliefs on a captive audience. And private prayer? Well, I couldn't see any reason to pray to a God I didn't believe in—a God that would grant favors to some and deliver harsh judgments to others.

Over the years, my theology softened and I started experimenting with spiritual practices. I became an agnostic. I learned to meditate. I began to practice Quaker discernment, learning to empty and open myself so that I could listen for deep guidance. Still, I was amazed the day I began to pray.

It all started in a redwood forest in the Santa Cruz Mountains of Northern California. I was wrestling with a major life decision and had fled the city for some stillness and solitude, hoping that a few days of silence and deep listening would lead to clarity. The answer to my dilemma surprised me—it was the opposite of what I'd expected. But along with that clearness came a surprising revelation: "You need a daily prayer practice."

"But I'm a lifelong Unitarian Universalist," I protested. "I don't know how to pray."

"Figure it out."

So I sat down on the floor, lit a candle, and said aloud something like, "I think I'm supposed to start a prayer practice, but I have no idea what I'm doing." What poured out astonished me—a long prayer of gratitude for all the people who had helped me get to this particular moment in my life. One by one, I thanked family and friends, teachers, mentors, ministers, doctors and other healers, support group members, and therapists. The list went on and on. Acquaintances. Persons whose names I didn't know but who had, unknowingly, said or done exactly what I needed in a particular moment. I lost track of time as I surrendered to the flow of names and faces. Eventually I realized that my prayer of thanksgiving was endless; there were far more people than I could ever name. When I stopped, I felt emptied, deeply grateful, and connected through time and space to an amazing web of interdependence.

This outpouring of names didn't answer my question of what a *daily* prayer would look like, but the admonition was strong, so I decided to experiment. I started with familiar words—a beloved poem that was really a prayer, E. E. Cummings's "i thank You God for most this amazing day." For a few months, I prayed this poem at the end of every day. I learned the words by heart. I tried to say them afresh each time, rather than simply reciting them, listening for which words rang truest and which were most challenging. Then came September 11. I remember sitting down that evening to pray, wondering how on earth to give thanks after such an event. I ad-libbed, saying something like, "It's really hard to thank you for most *this* amazing day. I *am* grateful for the 'leaping greenly spirits of trees' and a 'blue true dream of sky,' as well as blessed community at the farmers' market, where we clung to each other in shock and horror."

The spell was broken. I no longer needed Cummings's words. From that point on, my nightly gratitudes became concrete and personal: "Thank you for that parking space when I really needed it." "Thank you for the last loaf of bread." "Thank you for my getting home before the downpour hit." "Thank you for the breathtaking sunset." Some days were easier than others, but when I stopped to think about it, there was always something to be grateful for.

Eventually I started adding occasional requests for help. "Please help me to stay calm when I meet with my boss tomorrow." "Please help me muster the courage to say no." "Please help me find the words to explain what I mean." Occasionally, on a very bad day, I would shake my fist at the universe, invoking my inner Tevye, the poor Jewish milkman from *Fiddler on the Roof* who kept up a running conversation with his God: "Really?! What were you thinking? This is not okay with me!"

Who or what was I praying to?

On one level, I don't think it matters. Whether or not there was a recipient for my prayers, the act of praying was changing me. I could feel it. Gratitude spilled into the rest of my day, shifting my mood. Asking for help was powerful, both because it helped me to set intentions (e.g., "I really want to be calm when I meet with my boss") as well as to surrender a bit since the subtext was something like, "I'm scared. I don't think I can do this alone. I'll do my part, but I could really use a little help." Lifting up these concerns to a beneficent something bigger than me—whatever it was, whether it was there or not—lightened my load. Praying didn't abdicate my role or responsibility, but it did offer a feeling of companionship on the journey.

Another answer is that my conception of what I'm praying to keeps evolving. When I was a teenager, I rejected the favor-granting old-white-man-in-the-sky god and called myself an atheist. In high school, I mellowed to agnostic. In college, I read Emerson and my world shook. The radical oneness Emerson described was something I'd experienced as a child, but for which I had no words. What if I used the word *God* to refer to that sense of profound connection to the natural world and all its beings? More recently, I've adopted the stance that God is beyond human understanding, that anything we envision or describe is but a limited facet of the Great Mystery. At the same time, most of us need words or images to find a way to connect to Spirit. Sometimes I pray to a flow of compassion and wisdom, hoping to tap into this energetic river. Sometimes I picture myself held in love and light and protection.

But I'm getting ahead of myself. Back to my evolving prayer practice. I discovered that taking time every day to find *something* to be grateful for had changed me. I was happier and more present to my life. I found myself offering gratitude throughout my day. "Thank you for that car not hitting me." "Thank you for that golden ginkgo tree." "Thank you." "Thank you." "Thank you." Today, you can find all sorts of research on the benefits of gratitude. Back then, I was following a holy hunch. At some point, I decided that the one obligatory part of my daily prayer was gratitude. Everything else was optional.

I still got stuck, however, when someone would ask me to pray for them or when I wanted to pray for someone in need. In part, I hesitated because I remembered people who wanted to pray for me, when I was pretty sure they were praying for things I didn't want, such as saving my soul. But the bigger question was *how* to pray for someone else.

I asked around for suggestions, learning that some people pray by holding in their minds an image of the person they're praying for, perhaps surrounding that image with light. Unfortunately, I discovered that I couldn't maintain my visual focus. My attention kept shifting. More effective for me was a chant by Melanie DeMore: "I am sending you light, to heal you, to hold you. I am sending you light, to hold you in love." I chanted these words repeatedly with my women's singing circle, holding a different name for each verse. Sometimes I chanted these words on my own. That helped.

Then I learned Buddhist *metta* prayer. This involves directing loving kindness toward oneself, loved ones, neutral people, challenging people, a community, and the world, wishing the same qualities (e.g., happiness, safety, health, peace) for folks in each category. Again, I found it most effective for me to sing the words—outwardly or inwardly—and was grateful to learn several singing mettas.

Then I began an internship as a hospital chaplain, which upped the ante significantly. It was one thing to experiment with developing a private prayer practice that rang true for me. But now other people expected me to pray aloud for them, using traditional religious language that wasn't *my* religious language—terms like *Lord* and *Heavenly Father*. Also, as a Jew, I didn't know whether I could pray with integrity while using the words *in Jesus's name*. What to do?

I confess that I fudged a bit at the beginning. I asked patients and families if *they'd* like to say the words while I held the space (please, please!). Or, I'd start the prayer and then ask if they'd like to add something, which almost always resulted in them finishing the prayer by saying, "In Jesus' name, Amen." The gift of my passing the buck was that I learned from these experienced pray-ers. I'll never forget one man for whom almost everything had gone wrong—health, marriage, home, job. If anyone had a right to shake a fist at the universe, he did. Instead, to my amazement, he began his prayer with a list of gratitudes, thanking his estranged wife for visiting, the doctors and medical staff for their good care, the "lady chaplain" for coming by, and on and on. From him, I learned that regardless of how bad things are—and things for him were very bad—there is always something to be grateful for. From my many Baptist patients, I learned the importance of starting a prayer with praise, and of multiple voices chiming affirmations throughout the prayer: "Yes, Lord." "Praise Jesus." "Amen."

Eventually I got braver, weaving these lessons into a format that worked for me. I grew more comfortable invoking spirit in language that worked for my patients and their families, knowing how important words can be. I found a spaciousness inside myself that helped me to pray to a "Heavenly Father" or "in Jesus's name," knowing that these were manifestations of the holy that helped these folks connect to God. I developed wordings that spoke to people's deep yearning for a medical miracle while not setting up God for failure, praying for "whatever healing may be possible, healing of body, mind, and spirit" and that "God guide the medical staff—their minds, their hearts, and their hands—to deliver the very best care."

Meanwhile, to my great joy, I had discovered Jewish Renewal, a socially progressive, transdenominational approach to Judaism that emphasizes accessibility, meaning, and spiritual practice. I began attending weekly *Shabbat* (Sabbath) services, delighting in the ancient Jewish tradition of singing prayers rather than speaking them. I also grew to love the centerpiece of all Jewish prayer services—the *Amidah*, or silent standing prayer. After all that delicious singing, it was lovely to spend a few minutes together in silence. While it's traditional to pray the *Amidah* by whispering pages of words at breakneck speed, in Jewish Renewal, we're encouraged to spend at least part of this time lifting up our own words or simply listening. Before long, I put the prayer book down. I pulled my white prayer shawl over my head, creating a little tent of privacy in a sea of people, and listened for whatever might arise in the silence. I grew to love this moment in the prayer service—an island of quiet in an ocean of sound. The prayers it drew out of me were different from those I experienced in the quiet of my home.

To this day, my personal practice keeps evolving. I've kept my bedtime prayers, but I find that prayer has begun leaking into the rest of my day. On crowded subway cars or in checkout lines, I offer metta to the people around me, discovering that this practice helps my heart to open and my impatience to subside. As I drive through the crowded city streets, on the lookout for distracted pedestrians crossing against the light, I use a shorthand version of metta, simply saying under my breath, "Blessings" as I look at each person. For me, *blessings* means, "I wish you every good thing." Again, this simple practice softens my heart and shifts my annoyance. For distracted or aggressive drivers, I pray, "May you be safe. May your driving not harm anyone."

On my drive to the hospital where I work, prayer helps to prepare me for my day. I ground myself with gratitude and perhaps a chant of praise as I marvel at the beauty of the trees, the grasses, the sky. I set my intention for the day as I speak my chaplain prayer aloud: "May I be what's needed. May I be of service. May I be a blessing." I ask blessings for the patients, the visitors, and the staff, knowing how challenging each of those roles can be. I extend metta to a coworker whom I find particularly challenging. I've learned that forcing myself to wish her well softens my heart and renders me less reactionary.

As a final preparation, in ancient Jewish tradition, I invoke four angels who each symbolizes particular qualities: Michael at my right (reminding me that spirit is with me, that I do not do this work alone); Gavriel at my left (representing strength, courage, and healthy boundaries); Uriel in front of me (symbolizing a beacon of light, guiding me); and Raphael behind me (embodying healing and compassion). Imagining these holy beings surrounding me as I do the profound, sacred, and unpredictable work of hospital chaplaincy helps keep me grounded, humbled, courageous, and open.

Before significant meetings—at work, at church, or otherwise—I take a few deep breaths and pray for compassionate listening, for speaking our truths from a place of love. My favorite prayer is simple: "May we each see what we need to see, hear what we need to hear, say what we need to say, and do what we need to do. May we be guided toward whatever serves the greater good." There is no magic here, no supernatural hocus-pocus. Rather, the simple act of praying grounds me, reminding me of my deepest values and highest aspirations, loosening my grip on outcomes and opening me to possibility.

This is my prayer practice today. I fully expect that it will continue to evolve. By the time this essay is published, it may have shifted again. This kind of continual unfolding is one of the gifts and challenges of Unitarian Universalism. The challenge is that Unitarian Universalism offers no one right way of doing things—no requisite words to say or gestures to learn. The gift is the space for each of us to experiment, personalize, and find our own way, which can lead to spiritual practices that are vibrant and flexible.

In closing, I offer you a short prayer:

May you find spiritual practices that support you on your journey, through all that life throws your way.

May these practices help you to live the life you yearn for, become your best self, walk your talk.

May you find the courage to experiment with new spiritual practices, particularly those that seem awkward or uncomfortable at first, trying them on to see what fits.

May your spiritual practices evolve and grow with you, blessing you all the days of your life.

finding a teacher

wayne b. arnason

Waiting in the line of students sitting on cushions outside the abbot's *dokusan* (interview) room, my heart beat rapidly and the sweat on my palms did not match the unusually cool summer day outside. I was about to have my first personal interview with a Zen teacher. The senior monks running this "Introduction to Zen Practice" retreat had prepared us for this interview by encouraging us to think of one question to ask. The encounter would be short, like most Zen dokusans. There would be a little bit of personal exchange after the question was posed, but not a lot. For Zen students doing formal *koan* practice, an interview can consist merely of a recitation of the teaching story under consideration, an opportunity for the student to respond to a question or image in the story, and a response from the teacher. The teacher's response can be quite minimal, perhaps as simple as ringing a bell to indicate that the interview is over. The response can also be more expansive, with further questions or reflections about the koan before the student leaves.

The senior monks had encouraged me to treat this interview as an opportunity to ask the Buddha a question. Zen Buddhists believe that the Buddha mind is transmitted from teacher to student, as well as a belief in the common Buddha nature of all sentient beings. So imagining that I was about to ask the Buddha a question both made sense and was extremely daunting.

Finally, it was my turn. I stumbled through my recollection of the appropriate bowing rituals that begin the interview. I sat down on my knees and raised my head to look into the eyes of John Daido Loori, the man who would become my teacher. I spoke my name and my practice and then asked my question: "What do I have to give up to follow this path?"

Twenty years have passed since I asked that question. Because I am still answering it, I am no longer sure what Daido Roshi said to me that day. The best summary would probably be that I had to give up my expectations about what the path would be like and just walk on it.

I first began meditating in college, as the first wave of Asian teachers from Hindu and Buddhist traditions came to North America and began to teach. I started meditating within the context of a yoga practice and then plunked down my $100 and bought into the mantra meditation sold by Maharishi Mahesh Yogi as Transcendental Meditation (TM). Several years later, I experienced my first Buddhist monastic community and meditation practice. Although TM remained my go-to daily practice, I attended Tibetan and Japanese Zen Buddhist retreats occasionally and became a "bedside Buddhist"—that is, a regular reader of the pile of Buddhist books on my nightstand. My spiritual practice has gradually moved from the mantra meditation taught at TM toward *zazen*, the meditation discipline at the heart of Zen Buddhism.

Like thousands of other North Americans, I had grown up with a church affiliation and involvement but with an eclectic commitment to spiritual practice. My Unitarian Universalist church community provided me with many opportunities to explore different disciplines, and I did. I did my TM practice alone and never connected with any local TM groups. I did not feel the need to seek out or commit to a personal relationship with a meditation teacher until midlife. My thirties were years of family life, childrearing, and career building. I kept up my sitting meditation practice, but inconsistently. Even as I was becoming more drawn to Zen Buddhism, I was struggling with a stuck feeling, a combination of boredom and frustration with the meditation that had previously brought me joy and contentment. I decided that I needed to find a teacher. After a year of research and visits, I turned to a monastic community and teacher five hundred miles from where I lived for guidance and support in how to deepen my spiritual practice.

Why this extreme step? After all, meditation is possibly the easiest of spiritual disciplines to do anywhere. Books and digital media about how to do it are easy to find. It is eminently suitable as a solitary discipline. Why, then, would I drive nine hours each way several times a year to do something silently with a group of monks and students that I can do silently at home every day? To answer this question from within the Buddhist tradition, we must first understand that Buddhism is like a three-legged stool. It is supported by three "refuges," as they are called, sheltering the realities that sustain one's practice. The first refuge is the Buddha, both the historical Buddha and the Buddha nature, which is foundational to us all, our true nature. The second refuge is the *dharma*, the teachings of the Buddha. Dharma can also be understood to mean all the aspects of the universe and our daily lives in which we find the teachings present or illuminated. The third leg of the stool is the *sangha*, the community of people who practice together, not only in a particular place and time but throughout space and time. All three refuges are important, yet during much of my twenty-five years of sporadic meditation practice, I was missing a teacher and a sangha.

The *sangha* includes both the teacher and the community of fellow practitioners. The teacher, however, can be understood to embody all three legs of the stool of this practice.

The teacher is the Buddha in this time and place, conveys the dharma to the students, and leads the sangha. Not all Buddhist temples or retreat centers or sitting groups offer the presence of a resident teacher with a clear line of succession to a tradition of earlier teachers. This element was important to me when I decided to seek out a teacher, and it was one reason I was attracted to a monastic setting.

Coming to terms with the fact that I needed a teacher was not easy for me. I had to confront many old images and expectations of who I was. I am a grown-up. (Kids have teachers; grown-ups don't.) I was raised and continue to be a member of a liberal church tradition. (We build our own theologies.) Ultimately, what was hardest was admitting to myself that I didn't know what I was doing. In spite of all the sitting, the retreats, and the books, I really didn't have a clue what living and acting from within my true nature meant, without the intervening screen of conditioned thoughts and feelings that keeps me judging, analyzing, and planning. So I needed to find a teacher to help me with my chosen practice.

Within the many spiritual practices described in this book, the need to engage with a teacher can be obvious or hidden. Some spiritual practices are so easy to do (walking, for example) that the thought of finding a teacher might never enter your head. Other practices (playing an instrument, mastering a craft) obviously require at least an initial teacher and sometimes a full apprenticeship to achieve mastery over time.

No matter where your spiritual home lies, whether within Jewish, Christian, Unitarian Universalist, Buddhist, or philosophical traditions, teachers are available, once you accept your need for one. Over the past two decades, undertaking spiritual direction has become a vehicle for finding a teacher that requires no theological or participatory commitment to a religious tradition or institution. Developed within Roman Catholic spirituality, the skills of spiritual direction have become more widely available through teachers trained by respected nondenominational institutions (one example is the Shalem Institute in Washington, DC). Undertaking spiritual direction involves a process familiar to those who have been in counseling or therapy. There is a negotiated fee per session, and the spiritual director sets the terms for a minimum number of sessions and payment plans. Most spiritual directors, but not all, have a theistic presumption, and most are willing to work with anyone regardless of their theology. A question that many spiritual directors ask during the process is, "Where is God in all this?"

In some ways, choosing a teacher well is similar to any other wise consumer purchase. It starts with knowing yourself, as well as learning as much as you can about the teachers available. Personalities, teaching styles, and teaching traditions vary. There are frauds.

A critical reason to seek out a teacher—beyond acquiring knowledge or skills—is to make your practice *accountable*. We live busy, complex, and changeable lives. There are dozens of reasons why it is difficult to sustain daily practice over time. We are masters at rationalizing why we can't meditate. Being accountable to a teacher, a community, and a tradition outside yourself can help. Because Zen is understood to be a teaching that is conveyed mind to mind, "a transmission outside the scriptures," Zen teachers are part of a lineage going back thousands of years to which they are accountable. My first teacher, John Daido Loori, is an heir of several of these Japanese lineages. My current teacher, James Ishmael Ford, has both an overlapping and differing lineage from that of Daido Roshi.

It is not unusual in Zen to have more than one teacher, as I have had. In most forms of spiritual practice, sustaining a practice over a lifetime will at some point involve different teachers to meet a change in your own evolution or life circumstances.

Experiencing monastic life itself as a teacher is extremely valuable. There are many options for exploring monastic life and its practices. Although my particular experience has been with Zen Buddhism, Christians (particularly those in the Roman Catholic, Episcopalian, and Lutheran traditions) have long been aware of opportunities for study and practice within their monastic communities. Many monasteries within various traditions are open to lay involvement through structured group or individual retreats. Even though some monasteries house orders of monks who are exclusively either male or female, their retreats are usually open to people of all genders. A local congregation will help you find a monastic community that offers retreats or spiritual instruction.

You might expect monasteries to be places of quiet. Yet during a typical day or week, monasteries that are open to residential guests or that offer retreats and workshops will buzz with the activity of students of the monastery and inquirers from all over the United States. Most visitors will never be monks. They are drawn nevertheless to this monastic training center for its atmosphere, its structure, and the quality of instruction and support they find there, and by the fact that the monastery asks something of everyone. Even if you are simply attending a retreat and have paid a registration fee, you are nevertheless expected to participate in the life of the monastery, including its work schedule, while you are there.

Some students find their experience of practice on retreats so compelling that they consider formally becoming students of the teacher and the monastery. While monasteries have varying traditions, policies, and rules regarding people who want to explore the monastic life, most require a period of postulancy and training. Monastic vows are usually taken in several stages because the community wants each person to be very clear about the commitment being made.

The path I chose and followed for sixteen years was to become a formal student of the first monastery I went to in search of a teacher. As students, we committed ourselves to a Zen practice in our lives at home. We were expected to complete five "barrier gates" (five steps to help prospective students clarify their intent), sustain a relationship with a training director, attend two week-long *sesshin* retreats each year, and pursue our practice in each of eight different areas of training. The monastery also supported home practice through books and other resources as well as relationships with the teacher and training director.

Becoming a formal student of a spiritual training institution such as a monastery involves a demanding program of spiritual commitment. It is not for everyone. As a student, making time for daily practice, my most common struggle, involved getting up early each day for a clear space of time before any personal, family, or professional obligations could interfere.

When I was at the monastery, my practice could deepen in many ways. The opportunity for formal interviews with the teacher, the interaction with the resident monks, the chance to compare notes with other students, and the power of the *sangha* itself all contributed to a greater ease with and commitment to sustaining the practice.

Buddhist teaching begins with the idea of impermanence, and my relationship to the monastery began to change when my teacher died. I had great respect and appreciation for the new teacher I chose, who was one of his successors, but over time, I felt dissatisfied with my own motivation and experience. I decided to search again for a new teacher. That relationship became primary, and the residential experience became more difficult to sustain and less important to me. So I resigned my student status at the monastery. I may return to a residential sangha again, since it was such a valuable experience. I cannot imagine, however, being without a teacher. Even when the mind-to-mind transmission that Zen tells us is possible between a teacher and a student has happened, your teacher is always your teacher, forever.

questions for your consideration

◆ Do you have any experience with the kind of formal practice the author writes about? Have you ever considered engaging in such a practice?

◆ Are there any monastic institutions within the religious tradition you are connected with or attracted to that are nearby? Have you ever been involved with one or another, and if not, why not?

◆ Have there already been, or are there still, people in your life whom you might identify as teachers? Who are they, and why?

◆ What steps would you need to take to integrate the practice of working with a teacher into your own life?

how to begin an integral transformative practice

arvid straube

Most likely you are reading this book because you are interested in reaching a deeper and richer life. You sense that you can realize more of your potential as a human being and are wondering about what practices you can undertake to realize the next stage of your development.

Many studies have shown that meditation, in its various forms, is the practice par excellence for the deepest and most effective way to achieve deep personal transformation. New brain-imaging technology indicates that, with a regular meditation practice, we can actually remodel our brains. Practiced regularly over time, it creates a calmer, kinder, less reactive human being and generates a sense of thriving and well-being not affected by outer conditions. You could do well to make a regular meditation practice the foundation of your life practice.

But meditation on its own is not completely sufficient. If we are to develop holistically, other areas of our lives need attention. George Leonard, Michael Murphy, and Ken Wilber have coined the term *integral transformative practice* (ITP) to describe this balanced approach to human transformation. The premise of ITP is simple. We adopt practices that help us develop in four areas: mind, body, heart, and spirit. Practices of the mind increase our knowledge of the world. Body practices help us to be in touch with our physical selves and to keep our bodies as vital and healthy as possible. Heart practices cultivate loving and compassionate relationships with ourselves and others. And spirit practices bring us in touch with the unseen sources of our being.

Here is a list of **mind practices** (you can probably think of others):

Reading and study
Discussion and debate
Writing and journaling
Pursuing a degree or certificate
Taking continuing education classes
Learning a new subject or foreign language
Book groups
Study groups

Here are some effective **body practices:**

Strength training or weight lifting
Yoga
Pilates
Cardio training
Balanced diet and conscious eating
Tai chi
Qigong
Martial arts
Sports
Dance (including Sufi dancing)

Heart practices include those that develop self-understanding, enhance compassion, and improve our relationships with others and the world. Some examples are:

Psychotherapy
Dream work
Journaling
Art, dance, and music therapy
Volunteer work
Heartfelt service
Twelve Step programs
Philanthropy
Couples' work

And here is a list of some more traditionally recognized **spiritual practices**:

Meditation (there is a big payoff here)
Prayer
Mindful yoga
Sacred song or chanting
Sacred dance
Mantra practice
Worship and congregational life
Ritual
Spiritual direction
Spiritual retreats, guided and self-directed
Gratitude practices

So, to get started, check the lists of all four categories for practices that you may already be doing. Remember, to be a practice, it has to be done regularly and consistently. The goal is to have at least one practice in each category for balanced development. What's missing? Choose at least one practice in those categories that are missing and start doing it. Begin with a modest goal that you know that you can achieve. For instance, rather than telling yourself that you will meditate twice a day for a half hour each time, be realistic. Establishing a new habit takes at least six to eight weeks. Try ten minutes five times per week. You may well find that, with time, you will want to increase the length of your sessions. Having support helps, such as teachers, coaches, and spiritual friends or a spiritual director to whom you can be accountable.

Remember that you cannot really be spiritual by yourself. Because we human beings are social animals, we cannot really develop our human capacities and potentials unless we are connected with others. When we try to be spiritual on our own, we miss the checks and balances that practicing in community can bring. It is also difficult to sustain a practice without the support of a community. As the Vietnamese Zen master Thich Nhat Hanh says, "A lone practitioner is an ex-practitioner."

It may be helpful to think of the three "rooms" of practice, all of which are essential for a full spiritual life. First, there is the *prayer or meditation altar.* Whether you have a room or corner of a room for a physical altar or not, this is your individual spiritual practice, such as on a meditation cushion or chair, a yoga mat, or a chair where you pray. Then there is the *living room.* This is a small group of between four and twelve people who get together to help and encourage each other in their spiritual growth. Examples of the living room include chalice circles, covenant groups, spiritual reading groups, meditation groups, Buddhist *sanghas*, and Taize singing groups; the list goes on. Finally, there is the *sanctuary.* This is a place of corporate worship or ritual—a church, fellowship, or congregation. Here, you come together with many others to remember what is most important in life, to recognize each other's life passages, and to relate to a broader community of the spirit. Ideally, your spiritual life will be grounded in all of these rooms.

In their book on ITP, *The Life We Are Given*, Murphy and Leonard write:

> When wisely pursued, such practices bestow countless blessings. If we do not obsess about their results,

they make us vehicles of grace and reveal unexpected treasures. In this, they often seem paradoxical. They require time, for example, but frequently make more time available to us: They can slow time down and open us to the timeless moment from which we have arisen. They require sacrifice, but they restore us. While demanding relinquishment of established patterns, they open us to new love, new awareness, new energy; what we lose is replaced by new joy, beauty, and strength. They require effort but come to be effortless. Demanding commitment, they eventually proceed like second nature. They need a persistent will but after a while flow unimpeded. Where they are hard to start, they eventually cannot be stopped.

I am convinced that the wisest ways that we can use the precious moments of our lives is to develop our birthright of wisdom, love, service, compassion, and happiness through these practices. By dedicating just a portion of our time to these pursuits, we can acquire a happiness that is beyond external conditions. We will experience troubles and challenges, but beneath the emotions of the moment, we will have a sense of thriving, belonging, and joy. We can be the people we were put on this earth to be.

questions for your consideration

◆ Among the various possible practices the author notes, are there any that you have engaged in or are doing now? Are there any that call out to you?

◆ Of the four categories listed, are there any that you seem to be excluding for your daily life?

◆ How might you integrate a practice like this into your own life?

directed mini-retreats

matt alspaugh

Seven years ago, I relocated to Youngstown, Ohio, where I began a new ministry with the Unitarian Universalist congregation there. I was a brand-new minister in an unfamiliar region, far from friends and extended family. I needed someone to confide in, someone to talk with about my own spiritual growth and struggles. I was referred to Sister Barbara, a Catholic spiritual director who lives and works at Villa Maria, a religious community and retreat center.

In my initial conversation with Sister Barbara, we explored our faith understandings, seeking to determine where we might overlap—or even whether we overlapped. While she believes in a personal god and the agency of Jesus, she also finds process theology and mysticism central to her faith understanding. I have Buddhist leanings and a mystical humanist sensibility. We found we could work together just fine. I began to meet with her monthly for spiritual direction.

Over the months, we connected best on the practical aspects of the spiritual life: disciplines of journaling, dream work, and meditation. She often suggested just the right small spiritual exercise that helped me go deeper with some experience—"Why don't you play with sketching that dream?" or "You might try writing a letter to them, one that you will not send."

One day I asked Sister Barbara if I could expand my visit from an hour-long meeting to a full day so I could "make retreat" on the grounds of her spiritual community. She agreed, and since then I have tried to make every visit a retreat day.

Retreat Days

Once a month, I arrive at Villa Maria at 10 a.m. for my retreat day and spiritual direction session. I head to the empty sanctuary for meditation. This 1970s-era building, with its great expanses of fluid, impressionistic stained-glass windows, is often flooded with color and radiance. A bubbling fountain helps set a meditative mood.

After sitting for a half-hour, I find an unused room where I read and write in my journal for the rest of the morning. I review my journal entries from the previous month (however few or many) and reflect on them as I write an entry for that morning. At lunch I find an empty table and eat in silence.

The afternoon might include a walk in the woods or a walk on the labyrinth on the grounds. On cold and rainy days, I might hole up in the small library, exploring some of the Catholic mystics and liberal writers: Thomas Merton, Teilhard de Chardin, Richard Rohr. Or I might sketch at the Art Barn, a converted farm structure.

My hour of spiritual direction with Sister Barbara is the center of the day. We might explore what I've realized about the past month or where I'm sitting spiritually at the moment. After my session, I sometimes write in my journal about my discussion, continue reading or sitting, or merely wander the grounds.

These retreats are sometimes the most satisfying days in the month. I try my best to attend to myself, to turn inward, to discern what is happening with my spirit.

Create Your Own Directed Mini-Retreats

I have become an impassioned supporter of spiritual direction as a tool for people seeking to advance their spiritual growth. We benefit from a pattern of regular sessions with someone who can be fully present with us as we sort out our current place in the world and the direction of our next steps on the path.

In the past, people typically found a spiritual director by asking their religious leaders for contacts. Several online resources now offer help in finding spiritual directors. The largest directory is that of Spiritual Directors International (www.sdiworld.org). It also indicates the spiritual tradition of the director. Some directors work remotely, over Skype, Hangouts, or similar video applications. I once worked with a Unitarian Universalist spiritual director via video and was surprised how well the medium worked for our sessions.

Some people object to the term *spiritual direction*. Some directors prefer terms such as *spiritual guide* or *spiritual companion*, which more accurately describe their work with clients or directees. But the older term is most widely used. Some spiritual directors are comfortable working only within a specific tradition or theological framework, while others are willing to work with a more diverse group of directees. An initial phone call or meeting will help you discern if your styles are compatible.

Combining a retreat day with regular meetings with a director adds depth to the experience. I am very fortunate to be able to take a whole day each month for retreat. You might have to juggle your daily life commitments with your retreat time and spiritual direction. You might try taking less than a full day for retreat at first or make a retreat on a weekend day. Quite likely, you'll find benefits from retreat and spiritual direction and be able to deepen your commitment to both over time.

Schedule the meeting with your director at the best time of day for you. I devote some time beforehand to prepare, so my meeting needs to be late in the day. Others may find an early meeting can help them set the tone for the rest of the retreat.

I am also fortunate to have a retreat center like Villa Maria available to me. Even if you don't have such a center, you can craft a retreat day pattern of your own. You might explore what facilities are available. Friends of mine make retreat at art museums, finding their quiet and beauty the ideal frame for contemplation. Libraries, especially university libraries, can be other good spots for retreat, provided you are not overly distracted by the delights on the shelves. Perhaps a coffee shop or dining area can provide quiet refuge for writing and reading. Being outside and walking or sitting in a park, rangeland, even a cemetery can be restorative. Consider what you really, deeply need in your retreat space. Where will you go when you need to cry? Where will you go when you need to dance?

For most people, detachment is a challenging but important part of a retreat. Staying out of contact is a desirable but sometimes unattainable goal. I depend on people like the church office administrator or my wife to contact me if there is an urgent situation but to screen and defer other calls or messages while I retreat.

Being silent is a core part of my detachment. But it can be hard to be completely silent in a retreat space where other people are not maintaining silence. My approach is to follow what the Buddhists call "noble silence": I'm silent except when interacting with people is necessary—for example, to obtain my food at lunch. At times, I may offer a quiet greeting but not idle chatter.

Retreat and spiritual direction helped me stay grounded as I faced the challenges of a new ministry; they have helped me find the direction of my own spiritual growth. Yet, the idea of making retreat is foreign to modern American culture. When I mention my retreat days, people are often curious and perplexed, unable to imagine that such a thing is even possible or desirable. The idea of spiritual direction is also foreign, though most people can see a parallel between seeing a therapist and seeing a spiritual director: They are similar activities with different goals.

As a longtime meditator, I'm amazed and gratified that meditation and mindfulness practices have recently become popular in schools, workplaces, gyms, and even churches. These trends fill me with hope. I'm optimistic that the formalized solitude of making retreat, and the one-on-one companionship of spiritual direction, may also become ordinary components of the practice of serious spiritual seekers.

questions for your consideration

◆ The Unitarian Universalist minister Rev. Carl Scovel used to recommend that "one hour a day, one day a month, and one week a year" ought to be dedicated to spiritual practice. Could you see yourself dedicating time like this? (What about only fifteen minutes a day, a half day a month, and a long weekend each year?) Does such discipline and commitment appeal to you or turn you off? Why?

◆ Are there any formal retreat centers near where you live or places where you might go that feel, as the author puts it, "retreatful"?

◆ How might you integrate a practice like this into your own life? If that seems daunting, how might you start small and grow such a practice over time?

the greatest of these is love

susan manker

After church one day I was greeting people in the doorway, and an angel came up to me. I call her an angel because she said something that transformed my life and ministry. "Where is love?" she asked. "I've been looking through all your literature, and I can't find anything about love."

She never came back, but she had opened my eyes and ears, and I began to ponder the meaning of love as a spiritual practice.

Of course, I immediately found evidence of love everywhere: in hymns, in liturgy, and in the relationships of the congregation, but that was not the point. I knew where to look. I knew the people and this congregation I was helping to grow. The angel was a stranger, looking with a stranger's eyes, and she had left with her spirit hungry.

I grew up as a Unitarian Universalist minister's daughter (and minister's wife's daughter), so I went to church almost every Sunday. We children would often participate in the first part of the service. I heard the congregation recite the covenant, words you really don't hear anywhere except in religious services. All those people speaking words together make a profound impact on a young person's soul. "Love is the doctrine of this church," they said. I said. We said.

I took those words to heart at a young age, and in spite of not understanding the meaning of the word *doctrine*, I figured it meant "teaching." I knew nothing about the evolution of that covenant, the history of humanity's struggle to worship in freedom, to worship from the heart.

As a liberal religious teenager, I explored ideas with my friends. We took walks in the forest and wondered about life, shared our various beliefs in the dead of night in a circle around candlelight. I was seeking meaning and a deep connection to the mysteries some call God. And I believed what I had been taught about Jesus: that he was a great man who taught that we should love one another.

I was seventeen when I went to visit my cousin in San Diego one summer. As I got ready for bed, I turned and saw a Mexican oil-on-velvet painting leaning on top of the dresser. It depicted Jesus on the cross with bright-red blood running down his face from the crown of thorns on his head. It freaked me out and seemed to radiate evil, the opposite of what I had been taught. As I lay down in bed, I thought about all the evil things that had been done in the world in the name of God. And the question came to my mind: What if we had all been duped? What if God was really evil, and the devil good? How would we know? I got really frightened.

I wanted to pray, but to whom could I pray, if I didn't know which was which? I decided that I must pray to whatever, whoever, was out there or in me who knew what I needed. I placed my hands together over my heart in the way I had learned at Anytown Camp (an inter–high school brotherhood camp; I hadn't learned how to pray at church), focused on my third eye (who knows how I learned about that), and opened myself to whatever or whoever could help me in my angst.

However it happened, I slipped into an experience for which I had no words. The inadequate words are a knowing of infinity and eternity. I knew a oneness with everything and all time. With this came a sense of peace that has lasted my entire lifetime. A voice in my head said to me: "You will never be able to remember this clearly; you will not be able to describe this to anyone; and you will never experience it again." Then I think I went to sleep.

I didn't tell anyone about this for ten years until I learned in a seminary class that it had been a mystical experience and that many people have them. I was amazed that we have this other sense that might open when we're in a great state of angst, need, or revelation. That has reassured me when facing the trials of life and death. The sense that we are, in reality, all one is a great source of solace, hope, and love. I am you, and you are me.

I had not done anything special to deserve this experience. I was not seeking it. I didn't even know such a thing existed. It came to a relatively clueless young woman in her time of need. Every time I encountered people who were seeking God or enlightenment, it made me uncomfortable. I couldn't tell anyone this had happened to me. I could only imagine them declaring I was insane, lying, or had touched God. I shied away from all those imagined (but probably very real) reactions. So I held it close in my heart.

But I also felt that the Unitarian Universalist faith was missing a breath of spirit. The tendency in many churches during the humanist/rationalist sixties and seventies, when I was growing up, was to deny the existence of what we cannot touch or prove scientifically. I felt called to a ministry of accepting that there are mysteries of life, a ministry of keeping our minds and hearts open to the possibilities of realities that might be beyond our knowing.

I went on a spiritual quest, consciously exploring some other faiths. My brother had died the winter after my experience, and I held angry conversations with a God I didn't believe in, cursing that I had been born Unitarian Universalist and not been given easy answers, as I assumed everyone else had been. I didn't know then that everyone has doubts and wrestles with the great questions of existence, with God, with Gaia, with the Spirit of Life and Love.

I also learned that death can come any time, and to cherish every moment of life as best I can, and not just to love my brothers and sister and parents but to let them know that I love them.

A teacher taught me to meditate, which helped bring my body and spirit back into balance. I never really left Unitarian Universalism, though, but just expanded my experiences. When I married and had children, I felt as if I didn't have time for meditating. And I was embarrassed about it. I found that taking walks was just as healing and spiritual for me.

Over the years, I took up Thich Nhat Hanh's Zen Buddhist teachings on mindfulness: paying attention as much as I could as I went through my days—from appreciating my breath to being aware of my senses to noticing the multitude that surrounds me, and moving back to my own groundedness in body and spirit. I became increasingly aware of the depth of gratitude in my life, and I fell in love with, and memorized, E. E. Cummings's poem:

> i thank You God for most this amazing
> day:for the leaping greenly spirits of trees
> and a blue true dream of sky;and for everything
> which is natural which is infinite which is yes

A life of mindfulness and gratitude has been my spiritual practice for decades, along with the constant practice of maintaining balance in my life. But when that angel came to visit my church fifteen years ago, I turned and remembered my earliest teachings, the thread of which had never left my life: that love is the doctrine of this church, of my life, of the world.

Love embraces all these practices of balance, gratitude, mindfulness, and all that is good in the world. Love is what infused me in my mystical experience, and I have felt it ever since.

The thirteenth-century Persian poet Jalaluddin Rumi wrote powerfully and passionately about love, as translated by Coleman Barks in *The Soul of Rumi*:

> Love is the way messengers
> From the mystery tell us things.

Rumi was consumed by love, not just for God, but for his lover Shams. He drank and danced and wrote awesome poems that continue to touch our hearts through the centuries. Love can be an overwhelming state of being, whether that love is focused on a particular person, a god, or all of creation.

Rumi spoke of the alchemy of love, as translated by Fereydoun Kia in *The Love Poems of Rumi*, edited by Deepak Chopra:

> You are the master alchemist.
> You light the fire of love
> in earth and sky
> in heart and soul
> of every being.
> Through your loving
> existence and nonexistence merge.
> All opposites unite.
> All that is profane
> becomes sacred again.

Love is the transformative power of the universe. This is an ancient teaching: God is love. We read in the First Letter of John that "if we love one another, God lives in us" (1 John 4:12).

When asked which of the commandments was the greatest, Jesus replied, "'You shall love the Lord your God with

all your heart, and with all your soul, and with all your mind.'
. . . And . . . 'you shall love your neighbor as yourself'" (Matthew 22:37–39).

I interpret "the Lord your God" to mean what *you* worship, what *you* believe is the divine energy or the greatest good of the universe. "Your neighbor" is not just the person living next to you but all who live with you on the planet, including the plants and the animals and all life that is interdependent in our larger neighborhood of the earth.

We can then distill Christianity into three words: "You shall love." This love is so much more than the romantic definition of love that we celebrate on Valentine's Day. This is the compassionate, caring definition of love, the first definition in the dictionary. It's the theological definition. It is not necessarily something that happens to you either, as in Rumi's poems. Rather, it is something that you choose to do. To love with the transformative power of the universe is a spiritual practice.

The ancient Greeks called it *agape*, a term Christians still use to denote love of God and love of all creation (those may be the same thing). The Buddhists call it "kindness" and "compassion," and focus on alleviating the suffering in the world. It is a way of being that so many people of different faiths take up consciously in their approach to life.

Love as a spiritual practice is an act of transformation, of ourselves, of others, of the world. Anyone and everyone should practice it. Mother Teresa knew about this kind of love when she said:

> Love cannot remain by itself—it has no meaning. Love has to be put into action and that action is service. Whatever form we are, able or disabled, rich or poor, it is not how much we do, but how much love we put in the doing; a lifelong sharing of love with others.

I have struggled with feeling unable to solve the troubles that abound in the world. It helps to be able to preach about it, to inspire others to do what little they can. I remind myself and others that we are but one drop in an ocean. Like the admonition of the Taoist sage Lao Tzu in the *Tao Te Ching*, "If there is to be peace in the world, . . . there must be peace in the heart," we must focus on our own selves first, each of us, because then we maintain ourselves as healthy caregivers of what surrounds us in life.

Love comes first in our own hearts. We ensure, as much as we can, that we are feeding our bodies and spirits so that we are strong enough to feed some of that world we touch. And caring for our own families is important, to ensure that we don't neglect our children, parents, partners, or extended families in taking up the healing of the world. In caring for them, we *are* healing the world.

I once knew a woman who worked passionately to protect the Grand Canyon. She tried to work full time, care for her children, and did many hours of volunteer work for the Grand Canyon Trust. She also got sick. Her life was out of balance, and she felt inadequate to the task of saving our great resource. It was hard for me, as her minister, to help her entertain the notion that we can only do a little and that little should come from the heart, from a place of strength and love.

If each of us did our little bit, not one of us would have to work ourselves to death to save the planet. As Mother Teresa said, "It is not how much we do, but how much love we put in the doing." This is a profound understanding of transformative love.

What does it look like to love one another? A million people have written about it. As a spiritual practice, you start with knowing you are one with the world and know that a part of you exists in each person and animal and plant and life. This understanding of our oneness also forces us to confront our complicity in harming one another and the planet. The eternal questions of the meaning of life and death arise when we do this: What are we really here for? Is there existence after death? Does our oneness guide us in making choices, in aligning our values with our actions like the Buddhists who do their best to harm nothing? How far might we go down this road? That depends on each individual, without judgment.

Transformative love goes deeper than romantic love, which by itself is not enough to even hold together a romantic relationship between two people. Many wedding vows include the words "for better or for worse, for richer or for poorer, in sickness and in health," as a reminder that relationships require more than the sentimental aspects of romantic love. Life is difficult, and relationships demand a strong and everlasting commitment. Transformative love, which demands our compassion and caring even as it creates change in ourselves and those around us, is the love that holds couples, families, communities, and societies together. It will hold nations and the world together.

Many couples choose to include a passage from the First Letter to the Corinthians in their wedding ceremonies:

> Love is patient; love is kind; love is not envious or boastful or arrogant or rude. It does not insist on its own way; it is not irritable or resentful; it does not rejoice in wrongdoing, but rejoices in the truth. It bears all things, believes all things, hopes all things, endures all things. Love never ends.

Of course, we all struggle with these aspirations. Life is very messy. Anyone who has raised children knows this. There are many factors that can make life feel almost unbearable. Sometimes the transformative power of love is necessary for breaking commitments, for setting strong boundaries, and for letting go of dysfunctional patterns of living. Love can keep us going, but it is also what gives us the strength to let go when relationships are unhealthy.

Romantic love can end and often does. Divine love sustains all life and never ends. It is the infinite, eternal, transformative power of the universe. It is *agape*. Though we aspire to peace in the world and the elimination of poverty and corruption, there is only so much we can do. But one thing we can do is love. We can see ourselves in one another and find ways to help each other.

I give a lot of hugs in my ministry. For some people, that is the only hug they get all week. And I look them in the eyes and see the divine spark of love that is in us all.

Many years ago, I was talking with some colleagues about how we sign our letters. Some use "in faith" or "peace." Some use "sincerely," but back in those days, there was a television show called *Sincerely, Susan*. I felt silly using that. What I really wanted to say was "Love, Susan." I thought a lot about how the romantic definition of the word had taken over the meaning of love. I decided to take it back. Ever since then, I have signed my letters "Love, Susan." It is part of my spiritual practice.

questions for your consideration

◆ The author quotes the well-known passage from First Corinthians in the Christian Scriptures. Where have you heard this passage before—if you have—and what does it mean to you?

◆ What do you think of the idea that there are different kinds of love (e.g., romantic love, transformative love, love of self, etc.)? What experiences in your life could be seen as exemplifying the different kinds?

◆ Have you ever felt the kind of overwhelming love the author talks about, or the incalculable gratitude expressed in the E. E. Cummings poem?

◆ What were you taught growing up about expressing love, and how might that help or hinder a spiritual practice of love?

the silent singing alphabet or setting the altar

laurie bushbaum

It is Saturday afternoon and I have come to church, steeped in the silence of the granite walls while the stained glass whispers color into the darkness. I am here to set the altar for Sunday's service. While this may sound like a chore, for me, this is a cherished part of my week. My sermon is written. During the week, I have also been stashing away both ideas and objects for the altar. This is now the time when instead of wrestling with words, I can relax into deep and soulful play.

Even if it has been a hard week of ministry, with an unexpected crisis or challenging pastoral needs, and I consider skipping my preparation of the altar, I do not. The more challenging the week, the more important is this time. I know from years of practice that when I maintain my Saturday sanctuary practice, I leave each time inspired, with greater joy, a lilt in my step, and a renewed anticipation for Sunday's worship.

On a given day, I may prepare the altar with one gorgeous bowl raised on a pedestal, calling attention to the color or the function of the bowl. Or the altar may instead hold several woven baskets, all nestled next to one another, creating a landscape of woven textures. The Hmong textile art that hangs on the wall may come down and grace the altar with its outrageously bright colors skillfully coaxed into complex patterns. The white birch branches from my hike last week lean in the closet, as I keep my eye on the upcoming winter.

For my altar play, I keep a large stash of fabric runners and tablecloths on hand. I might use the blue one this week. Or white, with a silver runner. I might use a Mexican blanket as we celebrate Posada. Or a piece of red silk embroidered with gold and paired with a statue of Buddha to accompany the theme of compassion. A massive array of vegetables and flowers grown in our community garden. A dozen elegant red roses. A single, tall candle or tiny tea lights scattered across the field of green cloth. Or maybe the ornate silver candelabra a member donated on Easter Sunday, 1913.

The church is quiet as I gather my objects and fabrics. I flip on the lights in the sanctuary and meditate on the worship for the next morning and what I want most to convey. One week, the message is about the spirit of gentleness; the next, it might be the importance of fierce courage. Each Saturday, I ponder, "What am I 'holding up' for the day?" The blessings and challenges of being a community? Or is my message about the discipline of seeing beauty in unexpected corners? What colors, shapes, images, textures, and light will speak to people's minds and hearts? My spiritual practice is to pull myself deep into the language below and beyond, before and after words.

I am engaged in an old and beloved ritual, one that goes back to my childhood. I grew up in a rural area and disappeared for rich hours outdoors. I was in the woods or at the lakeshore or along the creek in back of the house. I gathered bits of wood, moss, and tree bark. Out of sticks and stones, pinecones and feathers, I created little altars everywhere. I was often utterly lost in time until I heard my mother call me or ring the dinner bell. In those hours, I was one with all that I touched. The air I breathed was distilled happiness. The sunlight through the trees and dancing on the water was part of the silent, singing alphabet of my enchanted world.

What I was doing then is not much different from what I do now, as I stand in the church sanctuary on a Saturday afternoon. Just as I did as a child, I am paying attention to material things of the world and letting them speak a message far beyond what they are. I am losing myself in the arrangement of common things to shape a larger meaning. I am listening for how one item next to another makes a never-seen-before beauty. I am touching the essence of flower or glass, color or form, and letting it move me someplace new. I am witnessing creation. I am creation. I am inviting others to come into their own soulful play, where the visual world carries us to the soul world and the boundaries between them blur.

The theme for Sunday's service is "Mystery." In my hand, I hold an enormous, whirled conch shell. The shell will go on the altar. Beautiful in its own right, the shell has other secrets to tell. It tells a mathematical tale about the universe. This shell is connected to the architecture of the pyramids and the Greek Parthenon. Its spiral shape illustrates the golden ratio, a special number found by dividing a line into two parts so that the longer part divided by the smaller part is also equal to the whole length divided by the longer part. As an equation, the golden ratio looks like this:

$$a/b = (a+b)/a = 1.6180339887498948420$$

Leonardo da Vinci illustrated the concept of the golden ratio and used these proportions in his painting of *The Last Supper*. This shell is just a shell, and yet it speaks of so much more. By putting the conch shell on the altar, I am saying and praying to myself, "Ponder all of this mystery. Go deeper. Can you see that this is connected to that?"

Last year, Carol, a beloved church member, died. Like me, she was a quilter and fabric collector. For her memorial service, her daughter and I decorated the altar with her quilts. A quilt that her sewing group made for Carol as she weakened from cancer was there, too. It spoke of love and connection. Our caring ministry team individually wrapped piles of precut quilt squares that we found in Carol's sewing room around packets of wildflowers, tied them with yarn and handed them out to each attendee of the service.

My father-in-law was an accomplished biologist and a skillful amateur potter. When he died, we decorated the makeshift altar in a Princeton University science building with three of his gorgeous, iconic pots.

What we put on an altar tells us about who we are, what we value, what we have touched, and how we might live and die.

The altar in church isn't the only altar to which I attend. There is an altar in my dining room, too, on which we eat our family meals. We break bread and consume the cycle of sun and rain grown into food. Here we speak of our days, consecrate our daily moments to a larger whole, promising ourselves to family, to gratitude, and to justice. I set this altar every night. Usually it has intentional beauty laid upon it, waiting for us to take part in its communion: a bowl of rocks, candles, a plate of tumbled glass gathered on a beach, flowers from the garden, homemade cloth napkins. What is on the altar always has a story, and our family story is then woven together deeper by the presence of what I place before us and around us.

As my children were growing up, I set this family altar with care because I know that children who eat dinner with their families have a lower rate of mental health issues, more emotional resiliency, and engage in less risky behaviors. But I set this altar because this is what I know how to do and what my soul commands me to do. I need to stop and breathe and feel nurtured by the food at hand; the beauty nurtures the deepest recesses of my being. Every day, by setting this altar, I have laid out, for myself and for my family, an intention of sacred place.

I grow both flowers and vegetables at home. While I call these "gardens," they are also outdoor altars. The gardens connect me to the earth. I am required to pay attention to the warmth of the soil, to plant seeds with hope, to pour libations of water, and coax life with a tender hand.

We have one garden in the front yard, right next to the sidewalk, where we grow carrots, lettuce, peas, beans, and tomatoes. Here, we invite the neighborhood children to help us plant, to visit often, and to harvest the vegetables when they are ready. A long line of day-care children often walk by to see how the garden is growing. They taste a cherry tomato or a sugar snap pea. They can't wait to pick the carrots and keep asking if they are "done yet." This altar is about welcoming our neighbors and creating curiosity. And like all of the other altars in my world, this one is about the invitation to pay attention, to look closer, to be open to the mystery and beauty at hand.

Right across the sidewalk from the front vegetable garden is our fairy garden. Here, a two-story fairy house, complete with itsy-bitsy shoes on the deck and laundry hanging on the line, calls folks to stop and see. In addition to the fairy garden with a little archway and tiny plants, there is a tiny fairy bicycle, a little wooden bridge, a rock pathway. Nearly everything is movable so that others can enter the world and arrange it to their delight. In the summer, my husband and I often stand in the living-room window and see people stooped low, looking, playing, perhaps wondering. We see children's eyes grow wide and smiles appear. That neighbor who was walking with his granddaughter to the hardware store just got ambushed by a fairy altar!

When I keep to the spiritual practice of setting the altar, wherever the altar may be, I am a better person. When I hold a gold silk cloth in my hand and place it on a hand-carved altar table that has served in this sanctuary for a hundred years, my petty concerns slide to the floor. I place a ceramic chalice, shaped of people forming a circle, onto the pedestal near the lectern. I imagine all the children who have been dedicated in this church, all the weddings that have been celebrated, and all the lost who have found their way here, and I am humbled. When the Christmas tree, which a church family gave in honor of a young daughter who died, is lit on Christmas Eve, I step into the pulpit and pray that my heart is set as the altar is set, with loving intention.

questions for your consideration

◆ If you are engaged with a faith community, have you ever noticed the altar in the sanctuary and thought of it as a part of the message of the worship service? Pay attention to it for a couple of months. Does it make any difference to your experience of the service?

◆ Before reading this chapter, did you have any spaces that you considered an altar? What about now?

◆ If you had an altar at home, what items would you place on it? Why?

enlightenment in the dressing room

jaelynn p. scott

For me, a spiritual practice is any activity that unites mind and body, is rooted in tradition, is entered into with intention, and communicates with a transcendent principle such as God, Dharmakaya, or Oneness. It is also non-oppressive and non-appropriative. We can create modern approaches to spiritual practices that are ordinary and simple and that honor the ancestors. We begin with a belief in the sacredness of ourselves and our world. Most contemplative traditions teach that sacredness can be accessed by all if we pay attention, practice, and remain persistent.

Within my chosen religious tradition, Tibetan Buddhism, my spiritual practice of clothes shopping and dressing, centered on the concept of *yun*, has been transformative. Over the years I've created spiritual practices in many aspects of my life. As a religious convert and someone disconnected from the tradition of my own ancestors, I've longed for authenticity in my spiritual path. Most of the practices that I've experimented with have been short-lived and lacked depth. But my spiritual practice of shopping for clothes has helped me find contentment in my body, has precedence in tradition, is highly intentional, and has opened the door of the sacred to me.

Unites Mind and Body

I've never been satisfied with the bland, gender-binary cloth-ing offered in most stores. Long before I began to consider my gender, the experience of clothes shopping was an exercise in conformity. There was something inauthentic about trying to align my taste and presentation to the few choices that were offered to me. The color and fabric of typical "men's" clothes offered in major retail stores are decidedly bland and rigid.

I have always preferred to appear graceful in my presenta-tion. I've always appreciated a compliment for wearing a cute outfit, but I've never wanted my clothing to draw too much attention. There was no grace in the clothing available and I lacked the boldness to step out of the gender-binary box and wear "women's attire." I would often glance furtively and with envy at the tasteful pastel and brightly colored choices in the women's section, which would bring back memories of trying on my mother's beautiful gowns, blouses, and dresses when I was alone at home. I remember the softness of the silk against my skin, the new sensations of fitted waists and open shoulders. My mother's clothing was spacious, light, and pro-vided freedom of movement. I could breathe.

Before my gender transition, I shopped for clothing out of necessity. I usually decided on what I wanted before entering a store. I imagined that someone was keeping time and that I was in a race to beat some imagined shopping record. My approach was to look down, go straight for the object, and evade pesky wandering shoppers blocking the path to victory. I tried to avoid trying on clothes at all costs. The dressing room triggered my anxiety—the tiny spaces felt claustropho-bic, hot, and stuffy. It wasn't worth the suffering, and I could return an item if it didn't fit.

Now, post-transition, I spend hours roaming the aisles looking for the perfect piece. In the women's section there are so many lovely choices. These choices had been right there all along, just across the aisle from the men's section, but I hadn't dared to make them. Now, I take my time looking for those pants that are long enough to fit me but that aren't too "manly" or search for the sweater that doesn't make my shoulders look too broad. I seek out the right pair of women's shoes that are my size and yet disguise the largeness of my feet. I try on everything, taking up dressing room real estate for hours, often losing track of time before realizing that the store is about to close. Sometimes I walk out with just the right thing; most of the time I walk out empty-handed but happy.

My budget requires me to shop primarily at thrift stores. The garments in these stores come with a resume and references written in the folds of the seams. They have served their owners well and partnered with them through love and tragedy, adventure and mistake. They were so valued that their owners have given them a second life. I conduct an interview with each one: "Who made you? Did you treat your previous owner well? Did your owner treat you well?"

My clothes-shopping experience is now exhilarating and joyful and leaves me renewed and ready to show up more fully in my life. It's therapeutic, spiritual, and political—an exercise in freedom and resistance. Through it, I resist my fear, our gender-binary culture, and the threat of violence against me, a Black transwoman in America.

I also feel responsible for balancing my personal needs with those of others by remaining mindful of my footprint on this delicate planet. The framing of shopping as a spiritual practice has helped me to find a balance between the laborious work of shifting my appearance and the goal of limiting my consumption.

Rooted in Tradition

I've grounded my practice in a surprising source, Tibetan Buddhism, whose practitioners have, since its origins in the fifth to seventh centuries, created techniques to help ordinary individuals access the profound in their everyday activities. In Tibet, a new class of Buddhists evolved who were neither monastic nor forest-dwelling yogis but regular working folks who wanted to practice the highest Buddhist teachings without giving up family and everyday life. They created or revealed practices that corresponded to a full range of activities, such as eating, celebrating with intoxicating beverages, making war or peace, having sex, and dying.

One such practice, introduced to western Buddhists by the twentieth-century Tibetan Buddhist leader Chögyam Trungpa Rinpoche, teaches an enlightened way to shop. In Tibetan Buddhist folk belief, an object, landscape, or structure may possess a certain quality called *yun* that makes it a power spot, a place of resonance and magic. Enlightened celestial beings and auspiciousness (good causes and conditions) are attracted to yun. Their presence in an object or place makes the principle of grace tangible. For example, Tibetan yogis look for yun in a field of grass in order to locate a spring. The grass points in the perfect direction, the soil is fertile, and the sun shines beautifully on the scene, revealing an ideal spot for life-giving water.

Yun can be identified in an object by the object's luminosity. Our eyes are attracted to it, and we get chills up our spines when we hold it. For example, a well-crafted shoe can radically change a person's entire appearance. Something shines through in the craftsmanship that tells you these are special shoes that are not only beautiful but also functional, an investment in the health of our feet. That "something" that shines through is yun.

To help his students raise their awareness of yun, Trungpa Rinpoche would take them to antique shops and have them point out an object they thought might have it. He would then confirm or deny its presence. Yun is not subjective, it can only be discerned by a trained eye, by someone experienced in a centering practice like meditation. When we slow our thoughts down, we are able to see things that were previously too subtle for our gross consciousness to perceive.

An object's yun is a product of the mindfulness and love, the concentration and passion of the person who created it. A hint that an item might have yun is if it is well crafted. However, not all well-constructed items have yun, and an object need not be expensive to have it. Yun is cultivated further with the appreciation and care of an object by its owners. The piece needs to have been handled with dignity over the course of its existence.

Entered into with Intention

Before I enter a store, I take time to center myself and cultivate appreciation. I often struggle with my desire to possess every object that I think has yun and have to remind myself that the practice is not about ownership; it's about appreciation. I take time to acknowledge yun when I come across it, and when I do purchase an item, I experience less buyer's remorse. As a result, my budget has benefitted from the reduction in frivolous purchases.

My relationship to my purchases has changed since adopting this practice. Dressing in the morning used to be a source of anxiety because my clothes never felt right. I would put on a shirt, then violently rip it off, angry with the lifeless garment, which I would often throw across the room or shove to the back of the closet. "Shame on that t-shirt for its lack of consideration of my needs." Defeated, and realizing that there were no other choices, I'd retrieve the shirt, close my eyes, put on the horrid thing and run out the door before I could see myself in the mirror.

The change began in college when I befriended a beautiful, tall drag queen named Jackie (not her real name) and moved in with her. I was attracted to Jackie because she lived unapologetically at a time in Mississippi when the threat of violence was ever present for LGBT persons. Her courage ignited my curiosity, and I began to question my presentation, my gender, and my fear of violating social norms.

Within the walls of our little apartment there was freedom and I began to understand that there was something about me that was like Jackie. Her confidence inspired me to explore different and nonconforming ways to express my gender: I began to get my nails done regularly, played with different colors of clothing, freed up my tightly held masculine physicality, and shifted my voice. The painful morning dressing ritual all but disappeared; I was beginning to show up as my gracefully effeminate, authentic self.

My family soon took notice. It was one thing to be discretely Black and queer; it was another to threaten a Black family's stability by not conforming to social norms. My parents had worked hard to climb the economic and social ladder. They were valued and respected members of their community, my father an entrepreneurial leader and my mother a corporate supervisor. Rumors and whispers about my gender and sexuality could threaten my father's standing at his Masonic lodge, his church, and his business associations. My mother, as a Black woman, had fought hard for equal treatment in her work. She would never admit this, but I knew she couldn't afford to have any "stains" on her professional persona. My parents had achieved so much in a part of the country that gives African Americans very little room to thrive, and I understood that my new way of showing up in the world put their life's work at risk.

Out of respect and concern for my parents, I made an unspoken compromise with them to be a "normal" queer who stayed within the confines of my gender. I promised them that "nothing has changed about me, I am still the son that you raised," knowing they could tolerate me being queer as long as I didn't publicly embarrass them. If questioned by their friends, co-workers, or fellow church members, they could have plausible deniability.

The painful morning ritual around clothing that had previously all but disappeared soon returned. Each day I was
forced to decide whether I would live authentically or give in
to fear. Every morning my spirit would resist against living
according to binary gender norms. My spirit was relentless in
its persistence, yet quite compassionate in refusing to give up
on me. It took many years, but one morning I just refused to
do it again. I forced myself to address the cause of my discon-
tent. I could no longer live this way. I no longer wanted this
painful ritual to dictate my days. I no longer wanted those
clothes in my closet. I believed there was a different way to
be in relationship with clothing that was healthy, loving, and
transformative, and my spiritual practice of shopping for
clothes began with this recognition.

Invokes a Transcendent Principle

The yun-possessing objects I encounter are a blessing and a
fresh breeze along the often painful and confusing path of
gender transitioning. The dressing room of the local thrift
store has become a sacred meditation cave, full of the presence of the deities of enlightenment, offering healing, love,
and wisdom.

I believe clothes shopping as a spiritual practice could be
helpful to others, since we all have our relationship to presentation and dress. Many, like me, struggle with the limitations
of gender-binary choices. Others of us are unhappy with our
bodies and wear clothes that hide our "unflattering" parts.
Most people I know don't have a very healthy relationship
to their clothes. They are resentful toward them or obsessed
by them.

To make shopping a spiritual practice involves transforming the way we think about our clothing, our bodies, and
ourselves. Engaging in even a little mindfulness of yun in our
shopping might also help reduce our consumption.

All spiritual practices are about bringing intentionality and love to the activities of our lives. They help us pay attention to the magic around us that can accompany us on our journey. You might find it at the altar of a temple—or maybe in the aisles of a clothing store.

questions for consideration

◆ Do you shop at thrift stores and antique shops? Why or why not? What attitudes do you, your family, your friends, or even society in general have about them?

◆ Have you ever encountered objects that display the quality of yun? Did you notice it at the time or only now, in hindsight?

◆ The author describes some of the ways clothing has enhanced or denied her experience of her authentic identity. In what ways do the clothes you wear tell the truth about who you are, and how do they obscure it?

◆ How could you see integrating clothes shopping as a spiritual practice into your life?

entering the labyrinth

leia durland-jones

Have you ever had a soul connection to a shape or image? That's how I felt when I first encountered the labyrinth, particularly the image of the twelve-circuit labyrinth associated with Chartres Cathedral in France. Because labyrinths are enjoying a resurgence around the globe, you probably are familiar with this image. When I first learned about labyrinths, I mistakenly thought they were mazes or puzzle-like paths lined with hedges. The labyrinth is not a maze at all, although some do have hedges or are lined with plantings. In the mid-1990s, when a colleague described the labyrinth her congregation was making, she expanded my understanding of labyrinths. Immediately I was intrigued and wanted to understand more about what she described as a single curving path leading to the center and out again. Her congregation was painting the labyrinth on canvas. It was designed to be used indoors yet was portable for use in a variety of spaces. Wanting to learn more, I tucked my new understandings away with hopes that one day I would have the opportunity to experience a labyrinth myself.

About a year later, I received a mailing advertising a women's spirituality conference hosted by the National Cathedral in Washington, DC. On the flyer was the image of the Chartres labyrinth. Something in me went "zing!" The image on the flyer was simply a silhouette of the Chartres labyrinth design, but to me it was like a magnet. I felt compelled to figure out a way to get to that conference and to experience the labyrinth firsthand. My soul connected to that image in a profoundly powerful way, and I was able to respond to the call of the labyrinth and attend the conference. I will forever remember my first labyrinth walk in the nave of the cathedral. Members of the Arlington, Virginia, Unitarian Universalist Church had made the labyrinth and loaned it for the occasion. While my first walk happened over twenty years ago, my connection to the labyrinth has only deepened through the years. It is central to my spiritual practice. I interact with it daily.

So what is it about the labyrinth that continues to speak to me through all these years? Something about the ancient shape speaks to me archetypally. The pattern of the labyrinth feels both familiar and mysterious. I experience it as simultaneously grounding and ethereal. Some say that walking the labyrinth takes you out of *chronos* time into *kairos* time, moving you from the regular rhythms of seconds, minutes, and days to the larger sense of *meaningful* time, sacred time. You have a sense of timelessness as you move from the other paths to the inner and center and out again. Although there are many shapes, sizes, and styles of labyrinths and many different cultural interpretations, something about the form of the spiral is echoed in all the various designs that both connect and transcend each individual one. The labyrinth itself crosses time, cultures, and theologies. I love the form and the way it flows. I love feeling my own sense of flow when I walk the labyrinth.

Perhaps one of the most compelling aspects of using the labyrinth as a spiritual practice is that it meets you wherever you are—emotionally, physically, theologically, and spiritually. There is no right way to experience it. You can walk (at whatever pace) or skip, run, dance, crawl, go forward or backward, or walk straight in and straight out, using the labyrinth in whatever way feels true and right at that time and place. Sitting by or with a labyrinth, either alone or with others, can also be profound. Simply being with the labyrinth form is soothing.

An elder in the congregation I serve would come to our monthly labyrinth walks and sit with delight in the stillness and beauty of the church social hall. She often remarked about the transformation of such a busy and vibrant space on Sunday mornings into such a sacred one. Sometimes she preferred a chair off to the side of the labyrinth. Other times, she asked to have a chair placed in the center. While she never walked the labyrinth, her personal experience of it was deeply moving, and those of us with her were ourselves moved by her experiences. She enjoyed what I call a sacred pause. This is what I receive every time I walk the labyrinth. This sacred pause is a chance to meditate or pray or be with whatever needs being with inside or outside of myself.

Walking a labyrinth is a spiritual practice that people of all ages can access. On my very first labyrinth walk, a young girl was on the path in front of me. She offered me the gift of witnessing her total immersion in the experience as she danced and moved with joy along the path. Watching her connected me to memories of my young self and to the wonder of experiencing something new with such an open heart. A gift of the labyrinth is that you can walk alone or with others and with the young and old and everyone in between. There is room for a multitude of expressions and experiences. I find this inclusivity heartening. The use of finger labyrinths—handheld labyrinth designs in wood, clay, or even on paper—make the practice even more accessible for those who are ill, imprisoned, or unable to visit or physically walk a labyrinth.

My congregation has three walkable labyrinths. Our seven-circuit outdoor labyrinth is available every day during day-light hours. It is a focal point for our congregation's weekly contemplative midday worship service. My desk at church faces a window that looks out at the labyrinth, and my gaze is drawn there throughout the day. Sometimes I see others walking, but often just the space and form catch my eye.

The labyrinth is a symbol for pilgrimage; it helps me as a traveler on my life's path to remember to pay attention, to breathe, to listen, to pray. When I walk a labyrinth, I am reminded of my connection to the larger whole, to that which is bigger than my understanding. As I walk, I often feel held by something larger than myself.

One way to experience a labyrinth walk is to approach it in three stages—releasing all that distracts or distresses as you enter the labyrinth, a willingness to receive insight when you are in the center, and reflection and integration of that insight as you walk the path out. I usually have no sense of great revelation, magic, or aha moment while on the walk. Expecting this to happen almost ensures that it will not. Yet I have experienced greater understanding of what I carry in my heart and my feelings, as well as increased clarity, a renewed sense of direction, and answers while walking or after a walk. And while I do find power in the practice of sitting meditation and prayer, using the labyrinth allows me to engage differently. The labyrinth acts as a homing device for my soul. It gently focuses my attention, breath, and body.

questions for your consideration

◆ Have you ever felt a strong pull toward a particular shape or image? Have you found ways to bring it into your daily life?

◆ The labyrinth is often walked as a three-stage process (releasing, reflecting, returning). How can you see that three-stage pattern deepening your spiritual practice?

◆ What question or prayer might you take into the labyrinth?

my cosmala

jon cleland host

The wind stirs the leaves around me as I feel the tiny, hard sphere with my finger. The tiny glass bead takes me back— long before city streets, before humans, even long before the first dinosaur's roar echoed across the landscape. Eyes! This little bead represents the first earthly eyes to see—the distant origin of what would become my eyes. I look around and drink in a vista of fall colors of red, orange, yellow, and more, so beautiful, so rich against the dark tree trunks. With the forest around me, I wonder: Can it be real that I can experience such beauty, seeing all these colors? What a wonder our sight is. Our eyes can give us incredible experiences and, in an instant, can capture many megabytes of information, all so effortlessly. From the humble beginning of a single light-sensitive cell hundreds of millions of years ago, our ancestors struggled for survival, gaining each tiny eye improvement, one after another. More recently, my immigrant great-grandparents worked hard to hack out a living, eventually giving me both this land to see and the life to see it.

I feel the gratitude, the joy for this moment for all that was needed to make it happen and for so much that would otherwise be easy to forget and take for granted. I look back at the little glass eye that was a window into this experience. It's a round bead, only about four millimeters in diameter, easily one of the plainest beads on my Cosmala. I continue on my walk in these woods near my house, my favorite place to walk, meditate, and think with my Cosmala.

Basics of a Cosmala

Like a Japa mala, rosary, or misbaha, a Cosmala is a set of sacred prayer beads. It is also known as Great Story Beads or a Cosmic Rosary. As a naturalistic pagan, I am grateful to my ancestors, a central part of my spirituality, and this is reflected in my Cosmala. A Cosmala uses beads to embody the incredible historical journey from the Big Bang until today, as shown by modern science, with beads for chosen events in chronological order.

What a history we have! Unitarian Universalism encourages us to freely and responsibly search for truth. That search—along with the wonder of childhood—opened my eyes to our history. Evidence discovered in just the past two centuries shows that our history goes back 13.8 billion years, starting with the Big Bang. From there, at the start of the multimillion-year time frame known as "deep time," stars forged the elements of our world, gravity pulled it together, and life arose here on earth. We are all made of the stuff of stars. Atoms cycle through our planet constantly, such as the gift of oxygen we receive from the trees, connecting us in one web of life. The evolution of life means that my family tree goes so much further back than to my great-great-grandparents, but through billions of parents, connecting me through parents and children to every person alive, to every animal and plant. For me, this erases false ideas like racism and nationalism. Astrophysicist Neil deGrasse Tyson summarizes this, reminding us that we are all connected to each other biologically, to the earth chemically, and to the rest of the universe atomically.

Perhaps best of all, this is real. As real as the food we eat and the air we breathe. With the tools of science, we've learned things that our great-grandparents could barely have imagined, and we don't have to guess at it; we can *know* it. Many new ways of seeing and dozens of ways of knowing how old something is have filled in the details of our past and present in ways far beyond traditional origin stories. Learning the broad outline of how we got here and some of the details of our world has given me what I think of as "deep-time eyes," which help me to look at the long story behind even everyday scenes around me. A Cosmala draws from this deep well of spirituality. Perhaps this kind of spiritual practice is what Carl Sagan had in mind when he wrote in *Pale Blue Dot*, "A religion, old or new, that stressed the magnificence of the Universe as revealed by modern science might be able to draw forth reserves of reverence and awe hardly tapped by the conventional faiths."

More than twenty years ago, two Catholic nuns invented the simple concept of sacred beads showing our history. They took the idea of sacred prayer beads embodied in their rosaries and extended it to instead show our origins, making a set of beads telling our history. Since then, many people have made their own sets, with different beads to show events chosen from our history. They can be as short as seven beads, or literally thousands of beads long. (An average Cosmala consists of approximately 100 beads.) Regardless of length, going from the start to the finish takes one through our history, highlighting chosen events in order.

I've made two Cosmalas. When my wife saw how meaningful the concept was in the lives of friends, she gave me a bead to use as the Big Bang, encouraging me to continue from there. I incorporated many events that moved me, resulting in just over three hundred beads. Because I wanted to take my Cosmala on trips, I made a smaller "travel" Cosmala about ten feet long, with just over a hundred main beads, and hundreds of spacer beads.

Using a Cosmala

You can use a Cosmala in many ways to fit your own spirituality. It has fulfilled many roles for me—a regular anchor
to my life, a source of strength, a sort of diary, a doorway to
deeper feeling, and more. While others may have additional
ways to use their Cosmala, there are some primary ways I've
used it.

Perhaps the most common way is to feel gratitude for
our ancestors, who are responsible for so many good things
in our lives. When you are feeling especially grateful for the
good around you, hold a Cosmala, reflecting on one of the
ancestor beads, and think of the gift that ancestor has given
you. For instance, when a loaf of baking bread fills the house
with that full, rich smell, you might touch the bead for those
ancestors who first kneaded grains into bread, who figured
out the best ways to do so, bringing food to themselves and
many of us today. Much passes us by without appreciation; a
Cosmala can remind us of the blessings around us every day.

A Cosmala can bring comfort in hard times as well. Along
with important support from others, it can remind us of the
wide span of our lives, of the good that exists. Our family dog
died last year and took a piece of our family. Yet, afterward,
my bead representing our ancestors who domesticated dogs
from wolves more than twenty thousand years ago brought
to mind that long story of the thousands of times a dog has
been a beloved companion to a person or family. The bead
helps us imagine the many times a puppy was a little friend-
lier than her litter mates and became a comfort to children
and adults alike.

More structured uses exist, too. When we approach the
festival of Samhain (October 31), I know that soon I'll hold
a Cosmala as part of our family's Samhain observances. A
Cosmala is a very powerful ritual tool. Sometimes I use my
Cosmala alone, or with the family, or as part of a local ritual.
I slowly feel bead after bead, looking back at that mountain

of love built by our ancestors. Many of these ancestors did not know me specifically, but that really doesn't matter. We think of our descendants—and of all future generations—with love. Even though we don't know their names, we hope to make the world that we've borrowed from them a little better for them. Many of our ancestors likely thought so too, at some level, even if not explicitly.

When you are traveling, a Cosmala can make you feel at home, no matter how far away you are. By holding one, you feel the connections spreading back from you, through time, across the continents, and you know that wherever you are, you are in the home of your extended family. That extended family includes all of our human family and, before that, our nonhuman ancestors and, from them, all life on earth, reaching every corner of our globe. A Cosmala reminds us that our seventh Principle, affirming the interdependent web of all existence, is so powerfully, literally true.

Bringing a Cosmala along when traveling on vacation or to spiritually important places infuses it with memories of family fun or the spirituality of the place you are visiting. Later on, during any of the other uses I've mentioned, you can retrieve that place, that feeling, that memory. Being naturalistic, I don't think there is a supernatural energy charging the Cosmala (although others might see it that way). Yet, that energy in my mind is powerful by itself.

Perhaps the most common use of any set of sacred beads, in any tradition, is meditative prayer. A Cosmala works well for this, too. Sit quietly with your eyes closed. Start at the large bead for the Big Bang (or Great Radiance), and slowly move from bead to bead, forward in time (or in reverse, especially around Samhain). Learn the beads well enough to distinguish them by touch. You can do this while repeating the simple phrase, "Thank you, ancestors," quieting your analytical mind. Other languages from your family tree can be used as well. For me, that includes French: *merci, ancêtres*;

Anishinaabe: *miigwetch, anikoobijigan*; and German: *danke, vorfaren*. Alternatively, I've also used my morning dedication words, repeated over and over:

> From the Great Radiance—stars!
> From stardust—oceans!
> From crashing waves—life!
> From the struggle to survive—awareness!
> I am . . . the dimly seeing, thinking Universe.
> I hear my Ancestors, who made me, who live in me.
> Together we call to future generations,
> in whom we will live.
> Today, as before,
> we make their world.

Making your first Cosmala is a rite of passage. When our kids were old enough to understand some of deep time and the spiritual significance of the Cosmala, we allowed them to make their own. When they can describe twenty events, by age eleven or twelve, they get family recognition (and a party). During the family celebration of their first Cosmala, the room quiets as they describe each bead from the start (the Great Radiance) through all their beads. They then add to their Cosmala as they get older, so that it grows with them.

The information packed into a Cosmala makes it a useful reference and teaching tool, a purely secular use. When the beads are laid out, kids (and adults) love to look at them and figure out what each one stands for, see the deep history behind us, and work for a just, healthy, and sustainable future. I've discussed my Cosmala with groups of all ages.

Making Your Own Cosmala

Assembling your Cosmala is a spiritual experience in itself. When researching the information for a certain bead, or even just learning the order in which to place several beads, you can find great joy being a part of our incredible universe. By picking (or making) beads for each event, you can more fully experience gratitude or amazement at that event than our distant intellectual knowledge normally allows. It reminds us of the connections in our web of life, of which creatures evolved into which modern lines, or of how the cooperative evolution of two or more species so often led to wonderful innovations. These experiences come back to mind when you meditate using your Cosmala or when you use it to show another person the creative power of our universe over deep time. As long as you use the correct event order, the exact dates aren't important. The overarching rule is that the Cosmala should be as accurate as is *practical*, remembering that its main purpose is to provide inspiration.

First, design the Cosmala. A Cosmala can have a small number of events (as few as ten or twenty) or more than three hundred. Depending on its planned use (meditation, pilgrimage, comfort, daily practice, portability), you may want more or fewer beads to be able to wear it as a bracelet or necklace. Pick the events first and then get beads to fit those events. You want a meaningful Cosmala, not just a string of the prettiest beads you can find.

Your chosen events should fit your personal spiritual emphasis. The list below shows some possible events, from which you may choose a few, and provides examples of gifts from each ancestor. (You can find additional lists, some longer, of events to choose in the links provided in the Resources section at the back of this book.)

The shading indicates events that can be considered as "Ancestors"—I'll explain more about this below.

Date[1]	Event	Gift from the Universe
13800 mya	Great Radiance or Big Bang (dates millions of years ago)	Energy
13200	First stars form as gravity pulls hydrogen together, countered by fusion	Elements carbon, oxygen, etc.
11000	Milky Way galaxy forms in gradual process	Milky Way
10000	Supernovae produce elements past iron (lighter elements already made)	Elements copper, gold, platinum
5000	Formation of our solar system, at least a third-generation star	Our sun
4100	Great rain; the earth cools enough for rain, filling the oceans	Water on earth
3800	Life evolves from replicating molecules	Cells
2800	Photosynthesis makes oxygen, turning the sky blue	Blue skies
900	First animals evolve (creatures made up of many cells)	Babies and young
435	Plants colonize the barren land before any other life	Salads, forests
408	First land animals, insects	Butterflies
375	Tiktaalik evolves and crawls onto land	Arms and legs
252	Permian extinction	A warning of extinctions
230	First tiny dinosaurs evolve and later become huge	Dinosaurs
220	Turtles evolve from lizards, getting their bottom shell first	Turtles
210	Mammals, and later, breasts and milk	Warm cuddling
148	Archaeopteryx: birds evolve from therapod (two-legged) dinosaurs	Birds

115	Flowers appear in cooperation with insects and birds	Flowers
65	Cretaceous–Paleogene extinction event—non-bird dinosaurs are wiped out, mammals dominate	Dominance of mammals
50	Whale ancestors leave the land and enter the oceans (Ambulocetus)	Whales and dolphins
24	Proconsul, our monkey ancestor	Minds that figure things out
20	Dolphins and bats separately develop echolocation	Idea for radar
3	*Homo habilis* makes stone tools	Tool use
1.50	*Homo erectus* tames fire	Fire and cooking
0.60	Cave paintings and carvings/symbolism	Art
0.30	Ritualized burial	Cemeteries
0.13	Humans work out languages, which diversify during migration	Discussion
0.10	Dogs evolve as wolves enter our huts, and we pick the nicest puppies	Dogs
35000 BCE	Mother goddess and stone circle spirituality	Stonehenge, spirituality
10000	Agriculture provides more food	Bread
8000 BCE	Development of writing	Hearing the dead
1342 BCE	Latest date (probably earlier) for first monotheistic belief: Atenism	Unitarianism
230 CE	Latest date (probably earlier) for the first expression of Universalism (Origen)	Universalism
900 CE	Arabic numerals invented; Al Biruni proposes ancient earth (shell fossils)	Numbers
1620 CE	Francis Bacon establishes what the Western world knows as the scientific method	Science

1630 CE	Galileo tried for his scienctific views, (especiallially Copernicus' theory of heliocentrism)	Heliocentrism
1670 CE	Newton recognizes gravity and describes a mechanistic universe	Understanding of physics
1859 CE	Darwin (and Wallace) discovers evolution and writes *Origin of Species*	Family tree of all life
1912 CE	Scientists predict global warming due to burning fossil fuels	Foresight
1929 CE	Hubble discovers other galaxies and the expansion of the universe	Expanded universe
1940 CE	Modern agriculture, vaccines, and modern medicine developed	Food and health for billions
1953 CE	DNA molecule discovered by Franklin, Watson, and Crick	Our unbroken thread
1969 CE	Humans land on the moon	Space travel
1970s CE	Global warming due to fossil fuel use confirmed	Efforts to reduce emissions
1980 CE	Carl Sagan gives us the universe with his television series *Cosmos*	View of universe
1990 CE	Internet invented, connecting us all and providing information	Communication
~2020 CE	Today	Today's choices
~2060 CE	Most energy is obtained sustainably	Sustainable energy
~2080 CE	Stabilization of world population	A sustainable world
∞	The future	Our actions will determine this

1. The dates start in units of millions of years ago (mya); then around 0.1 mya, they switch to the conventional dating of Before Common Era (BCE) and Common Era (CE).

After you've designed your Cosmala, get your beads. You can obtain the *main beads* (event beads) in a number of ways. A craft or bead store will have many different beads that will fit your events perfectly. You can also make beads yourself for events that are hard to find beads for by using Sculpey clay or something similar and drilling a hole through it. I have made several beads by drilling a hole in an object, including my bead for the invention of electronics (an actual transistor) or my bead for stone circle spirituality (a small stone I found near an ancient stone circle). You can use special substances, too, like my bead for the formation of radioactive elements by supernovae, which glows in the dark. Several of my beads have been signed, like the bead for our last common ancestor with chimpanzees, which is signed by Jane Goodall, or the bead for the asteroid that killed off the dinosaurs, a tektite signed by Walter Alvarez.

I use small beads both as decorative *spacers*, as well as to mark time. Each spacer bead counts for, say, a million years, a thousand years, and so on, depending on color, though many people prefer to use them more simply as spacers without year values. You can encode other information in the spacer beads as well; I used black spacer beads on either side of any beads that represent mass extinctions. Gratitude for my ancestors is central to my spirituality, so I have denoted ancestors (both human and those before humans, all the way back to stars) using a clear spacer bead on either side of any bead that represents an ancestor. I include different types of ancestors (chemical, biological, intellectual, etc.). This is a small act of reverence. Almost everything contributed to our modern world, and that in itself is spiritual, reminding me of how interconnected we are.

Use strong cord to keep the Cosmala from breaking and spilling beads. However, with small kids in the house, and as a paranoid father, I worry about accidental strangulation. So I strung my home Cosmala with weak (fifteen-pound test) hemp cord. When working on a Cosmala, I never leave the larger beads out where they could be choking hazards. I strung my travel Cosmala with strong steel beading cord, with magnetic clasps every foot or so that open if any significant force is applied. Also, I added clasps every foot or so (on all our family Cosmalas) to make it easier to update or add beads. Then the whole Cosmala doesn't have to be restrung as it grows or changes with your spiritual growth.

My home Cosmala is on the wall as a constant part of our family spirituality, along with other family Cosmalas. We have decorative bags to keep each in and pieces of foam to wrap them around (especially useful for my travel Cosmala).

The process of evolution itself shows that the best creations are often made by starting in one form and making small, incremental improvements to fit each niche, just as our own spiritual practices often grow by small steps. After my first, basic Cosmala, I then added new features to fit my spiritual growth. It is critical to have a bead for the future and to think about how we would explain to our ancestors what we are doing to make a better world for future generations. Additional beads for hopeful future events are a good idea as well. In the same way, I hope that your own spiritual practices grow to keep you fulfilled and energized.

questions for your consideration

◆   What events, in both our larger history and your own life, jump out as important to you personally? Why?

◆   What do you think of spiritual practices (such as the Cosmala) that include touching physical objects? Do you prefer practices that are word-focused or sense-focused? Why do you think that's true?

◆   Do you think about questions like, "How did I get here?" and "What is my role in the unfolding of the universe?" Do you think these have a place in a spiritual practice?

practices born in play

making magical moments and letting them go

lynn m. acquafondata

Some of the most profoundly connected spiritual moments just happen. The light filters a certain way through a tree into a clearing in the woods, connecting earth and sky in brilliance. A piece of music fills the heart, becoming all of existence, lingering in the silence after the last note. A child says something that channels the wisdom of ages, filling an older person with a sense of awe and connection.

When each moment ends, it can never return except as a treasured memory. The passing aspect of these occurrences adds to their specialness and beauty and invests them with a sense of mystery, wonder, and longing.

No one can make these moments happen, though we can seek them out by going to particular places at certain times, such as a lake at sunrise or sunset. We can also seek them out by preparing ourselves internally because spiritual moments involve a relationship between an individual and all that exists. Two people can experience the very same occurrence in dramatically different ways.

Bubble meditation provides a tool to create a unique, fully aware, but passing moment. This spiritual practice brings the

past and future into the present, focuses attention and awareness, and then assists in the act of letting go.

The practice itself is fairly simple. It involves opening a
bottle of children's soap bubbles, taking out the plastic wand,
and blowing bubbles while focusing on aspects of life for
which you are thankful, troubled, regretful, and hopeful.

Three principles underlie the practice: focus on the now,
living in transience, and a spirit of play.

Focus on the Now

I begin the practice by thinking about an aspect of life that I
am thankful for today and naming it. I slowly blow a bubble.
As it grows, I reflect on that person, place, event, or opportunity and imagine the bubble holding my gratitude. I may
continue the practice by reflecting on more things I'm thankful for, or I may move to naming something that troubles or
disturbs me today. That could be something personal that
I grieve or a situation that triggered anger in me. It could
be something in the world that breaks my heart. Again the
bubble grows into a mini spherical mirror, containing what I
named. It captures that thought, emotion, or recollection of a
moment in time and holds it there in front of me in a fragile,
glistening globe reflecting my own image with streaks of rain-
bow colors if it catches the light at a certain angle.

One bubble feels light and hopeful as it mirrors my goals
or fantasies for personal or professional success in the future.
Another stirs fear and agitation as it portrays an ominous
prediction for the coming week or year.

I manifest each thought and emotion that comes to me
with bubbles, not denying or pushing away the unpleasant
ones but inviting them one by one to expand as I watch
before I blow them away. In the midst of pleasure, staying
in the moment usually comes easily, unless it also taps into
sorrow or guilt. But when I recall emotional pain, anxiety,

or sadness, or am in the midst of it, I sometimes feel the urge to deny, push away, or block out the feelings. Bubbles help to ease my impulse to flee from this moment because they represent innocence. They generally don't stir up uncomfortable past memories, and they don't last long. (If you have an unpleasant childhood memory involving bubbles, this probably isn't the best meditation for you.)

The present moment with all of its thoughts and feelings is the most crucial time. It is the point of transition from yesterday to tomorrow. It is the only moment we can know fully. It is the only moment we can exert some control over. It matters that we learn to focus in the now. But in our society, we have found endless ways to avoid knowing and experiencing the now, including electronic distractions, drugs and alcohol, continual work and activity, and constant chatter. Why do people avoid the now? Some of us fear that this moment isn't what we had hoped it would be. Others realize that living right now means acknowledging uncomfortable situations or experiencing unpleasant feelings.

Living in Transience

With the bubble meditation, I immerse myself fully, but temporarily, in the power of a life event from the past or future that affects me today. I bring an image to mind, feel and name the emotions, and pay attention to the physical sensations I experience. I focus this energy toward a film of soapy water on a plastic wand, blow all that I hold inside me into a bubble, and then watch as it glides away and pops. Sometimes it bursts quickly, sometimes it lingers first, but no bubble lasts more than a passing moment.

Without bubbles, I tend to cling to one thought or emotion and go over and over it for hours, days, and weeks. But bubbles are transient, ephemeral—I call them "globed-shaped mirrors that move." You simply can't hold on to a bubble!

Each one floats away and pops. Some days, the bubbles drop quickly to the ground. Some days, they drift through the air, disappearing at a distance. Did that joyous recollection float forever or burst in a passing instant?

Life also moves. Bubbles are a metaphor for life, reminding me each day that though I cling to the illusion of stability and predictability, life changes in every moment. Our lives are like a path on a long journey starting at birth and leading to death with many happenings along the way. Nothing stays exactly the same. It helps to know the path, to look back and remember, to look forward and imagine and dream what might be coming. But if we linger in one place for too long, the place itself changes. If we turn around and try to walk backward in time, the people and places are no longer truly there. If we could enter a time machine and propel to the future, we would completely lose the path.

Bubbles connect to human frailty, too. In a typical bubble meditation, the bubbles aren't intentionally destroyed. They are fragile. They will burst. My own vulnerability floats with my breath into each bubble. I can create a group of bubbles holding the emotional content of a particular situation or event, and they will blow away and pop. But this doesn't mean I have finished processing that situation and it miraculously disappears. I may blow bubbles for the same hope, fear, or regret daily for a long time. Each time, they blow away and pop. For that instant, they are gone and that matters.

Spirit of Play

Often I find myself focusing on the serious side of life. Other forms of meditation can become a chore, with me as the taskmaster. But blowing bubbles is, at heart, child's play, and no amount of analysis and theologizing about the practice can change that.

I create the moment by opening a can of bubble solution and blowing. Each session unfolds in its own way, depending on weather conditions, the quality of the soapy water, and the way I release my breath. Many tiny bubbles may form or one big one. Bubbles may move away in the direction of the wind and last a full minute or two, or they may hover close and pop quickly. On a rainy day, bubbles sometimes land in a puddle or on a film of water and float for a time before disappearing. I treasure the day when a big bubble landed on my dog's neck and lingered. She kept on sniffing the air and listening to sounds in the distance as though nothing had changed, but I knew she had become a fairy princess dog.

I created this practice to tap into the child within who loves simple, lighthearted pleasures. I can get so wrapped up that the whole world transforms for a time into the magic of a cloud of bubbles. That child brings healing to the struggles of life. In the midst of grief, healthy children who don't fully grasp the past and the future can let go of the intensity of sorrow to laugh, play, and engage in daily life in ways that adults often find elusive. Some of my most treasured moments have come when I could channel this innocence to smile or laugh or accept a quick blast of joy in the midst of a situation that primarily brought heartbreak or disillusionment. Like a child's game, this meditation has a structure and a time limit that contains its unpredictable aspects, creating safety and an overarching stability.

This bubble practice teaches my heart to seek the child within no matter what happens around me and to trust that she will be safe to express herself. Even when I'm closed too tightly to let her out, I know the child is there, waiting to play. When I yearn for yesterday and pine for tomorrow, I hold out the bubble wand, breathe deeply, and watch the air release through soapy water into the rainbow-colored bubbles. The game brings joy to life, reminding me to find time to smile and let myself feel light for a moment, whether life feels challenging or uplifting.

When I want to cling to one point of time in the past or present, I breathe deeply, and let my breath extend through soapy water and a wave of the wand to a moment of magic that holds me here now, the only point in time where I can access the power of transformation to bring about the future.

I generally choose to blow bubbles at the end of the day on the back porch in the dark as a final blessing before going to sleep. But, secretly, I keep my practice quiet and cloaked in the night for reasons other than simple closure to the day. No one who happened to glance over and notice me would understand that this activity is profound. I suspect my neighbors might label me as eccentric if I engaged in this practice in the front yard during the day. They wouldn't say, "How delightful! She has found a way to focus in the now, to accept transience, and to tap into a spirit of play!" No, I imagine they might wonder about my state of mind. The child within aspires to the day (a decade or two from now) when I'll wear a silly hat just because I like it and blow my bubbles in the front yard, crying and laughing without a care about who says what. That's when my practice will deepen to its fullest.

Bubble Meditation Basics

Buy a small jar of bubbles containing a plastic wand. Go outside. The practice can be done in any weather. If you don't want to be outside, try it in a bathroom, a garage, or an unfinished basement. You can do the practice by yourself or with a family or a children's class. It is appropriate for all ages.

- ◆ Think of something you are thankful for today, something big or a simple passing pleasure, like a stranger smiling as you walked by. Blow a bubble as you think about this. Watch the bubble blow up, float away, and pop. Do this a couple more times.

- Think of something that is troubling you today or an area or aspect of life around which you hold negative energy. Blow a bubble to represent this thought, event, or person. Watch it enlarge, float away, and pop. Name two or three more stresses or fears, or name several aspects of one particularly difficult situation or event.
- Think of something from today that you regret or wish had been different. Blow a bubble as you think about this longing or regret. Watch the bubble expand, float away, and pop. Repeat for one or two more regrets.
- Think of something you hope for or are working toward. Blow some bubbles.
- Blow some bubbles just for fun!

Bubble Mechanics and Potential Pitfalls

From time to time, bubbles don't form as planned. I might blow and blow and just can't make a bubble. Then I realize that like the rest of life, bubbles must adhere to the rules of science. They are made of a particular material that we use in a variety of environments, each of which affects the material.

Bubble solutions are made of detergent, water, and glycerin. The proportions of these ingredients affect the quality of the bubbles because they affect the surface tension of the soap film that forms the bubbles. However, you can't tell the proportions of these ingredients when you buy bubble solution in the store.

If your bubbles aren't blowing correctly, try a different brand of bubble solution or make a homemade solution using distilled or deionized water. How and whether bubbles form varies based on a combination of factors, including the speed of the air directed at the tool holding the soap film, the size of the tool, and the distance between the source of air and the film of soapy water.

If your bubbles don't form, try:

+ blowing air at different speeds
+ changing the focus of the air flow
+ changing the distance between your mouth and the bubble wand

Bubbles last longer on cold days and can even freeze, though they will break when they hit the ground. They last longer when humidity is high and will pop quickly when the air is dry because of how fast the film of soap evaporates in different conditions. If the temperature and humidity aren't conducive to forming bubbles, try it again on another day or in a different location.

questions for your consideration

♦   What other creative ways of meditating on impermanence, in addition to blowing bubbles, can you
   think of?

♦   Have you ever sought "the child within" in other
   ways?

♦   What are some other practices that help you focus
   on the "now"?

instagram as spiritual practice

cynthia cain

Wendell Berry—one of the wisest among us, a fellow Kentuckian, and beloved essayist and poet—has cautioned us about the overuse of the camera. In "The Vacation" he writes,

> Once there was a man who filmed his vacation.
> He went flying down the river in his boat
> with his video camera to his eye, making
> a moving picture of the moving river . . .
> [At the end of his vacation,]
> With a flick of a switch, there it would be.
> But he would not be in it. He would never be in it.

We're regularly reminded of the hazards of giving in to the lure of social media. It's an addiction. It deadens the imagination. I have read that it can even be bad for your career.

Hence, it may seem counterintuitive to suggest a social media app as a spiritual discipline. Used for many purposes, Instagram would appear to be everything a spiritual discipline is not. This program, which must be downloaded onto your phone and then works by allowing you to choose filters, frames, and other special effects for your photographs and to share them with other Instagram followers to whom you've allowed access, has millions of users worldwide and links with Facebook and other social media. The proliferation of selfies and the incessant documentation of people's travels, material acquisitions, and superior home decorating can become weapons of self-promotion and self-aggrandizement that ultimately wound the poster and the viewer. They can also reduce our public image to a litany of things, resulting in what Martin Buber named the I-Thou as opposed to the I-It relationship with the world.

Nonetheless, I use Instagram, and I do consider it a spiritual discipline.

This medium was perfect for a way of encountering the world when I prepared a presentation for the final project in my spiritual direction studies. I wanted to highlight the many ways that my studies had benefited my own life and to do so visually. Over the months leading up to the closing ceremony, I used my Android phone to photograph ordinary things that I encountered throughout the day. I snapped pictures of things that spoke to me of the many dimensions of Jungian dream work: shadows, light, clouds, water, and dream-like scenes that called to me. I stopped my car regularly to stalk birds, stare at trees, fences, fields, and doors, each of which seemed to underscore something I'd learned in my two years' study. God's inscrutability, boundaries, walls that we build, family systems, archaic and ancient symbols of what Jung called the collective unconscious connecting humanity—I encountered each in concrete ways in the world I traveled through each day.

When I finished my studies, I realized that I would miss the practice if I were to stop. The practice involves looking carefully at everything I pass, seeing within it the light of the holy, noticing beauty even in the broken, old, and careworn, and stopping my day to celebrate as I decide upon an angle from which to snap a photo. These aspects of my day have become equivalent to stopping and praying or to pausing and breathing.

I read a cartoon recently in which a middle-aged man asks, "Can you believe there was once a time when we didn't take pictures every day?" I took time to remember. Absolutely! Digital cameras, iPhones, and Android phones make this incessant snapping of pictures both a joy and a burden. It can be a downright annoyance to have to line up for photos at every gathering and wait until someone takes a picture with each phone or to have to stop and pose or wait while your traveling companion takes pictures of each landmark you pass.

I try to keep my Instagram practice to the times when I'm alone (and as an itinerant, oft-traveled, semi-active minister, there is a lot of alone time), but I've discovered that the scanning, the observing, and the framing of that perfect shot continues even when I don't stop to take a photo to be uploaded later. I'm pretty certain this is because I'm practicing some other spiritual disciplines that span many faith traditions and that are timeless and proven to be successful: gratitude, stopping/pausing, and deep love.

Many have found gratitude practice to be of inestimable value, such as those in Twelve Step programs. They will tell you without hesitation that only by daily thanking God-as-they-understand-God for all that is good do they stay sober. It is absolutely clear to them that focusing on the negative will lead them back to drinking or drugs. Another place to find gratitude is in the traditional Black church. Prayers there often begin with a litany of thanks to God for the simplest gifts, starting with "I woke up today, God. Thank you."

Stopping throughout the day to pause and pray or reflect evokes Muslim and Buddhist traditions. When in Turkey several years ago, I thrilled to the sound of the *muezzin* calling folks to prayer throughout the day. Likewise, while on Buddhist retreat, the sound of the gong reminds us of our call to stop, breathe, and move slowly to the meditation hall, or *zendo*. These interludes that bring us back to our connection with being itself, with creation, are the ways we carry our spiritual lives with us rather than leave them on the cushion, the church pew, or the yoga mat.

By "deep love," I mean the kind of love that the Greeks called *agape*. This love goes beyond human affection or even filial adoration. It transcends anything we feel in our human relationships because it includes the holy. Even agnostics experience this kind of love, although they may call it mystery, wonder, awe, or simply curiosity. It takes a stance of joy and delight at the vast array of textures, colors, patterns, life forms, and mutations that we encounter daily. This beauty is not only observable in nature or in the country, but in the city as well, and in human faces, smiles, bodies, art, architecture, and even in food. Celebrating magnificence and splendor or just symmetry and simplicity provides a cushion of joy that helps me to absorb and balance the lashes of pain and despair that too often come from the world, and sometimes from my immediate surroundings, from people and things I can't control.

Instagram practice is not my only spiritual practice. I do some yoga and sit in Buddhist meditation daily. I have a Christian/Buddhist teacher with whom I meet for spiritual direction, and I attend retreats when I am able. I read and listen to books and tapes to bolster my spirit. I love to prepare food and to listen to music from many traditions and genres. But my Instagram practice is one that I can take with me when I travel or practice at home on my farm.

I can share my moments of insight and reverence with others simply by clicking a few buttons on my phone. I share them on the Instagram platform without regard for who will see them, but with awareness that they are meant for "someone/ones" else. To me this means that they are art. Art, be it poetry, literature, or visual representation such as painting or photography, is created for the other, and ultimately for the world and for God. The knowledge that my photos will be observed and shared, perhaps appreciated, brings a level of respect and sanctity to what I do that would otherwise not exist. My pictures are more than a hobby; they, like sermons, are a creation and an offering, whether for an audience of one or one thousand. In sharing these images, these moments, my wish is that others find a moment of respite, of wonder, and of gratitude in the midst of a chaotic and sometimes disheartening world.

questions for your consideration

◆ How often do you currently use your camera (whether as part of your cellphone or not)? How do you use it? What kinds of pictures do you take?

◆ Do you find yourself scanning, observing, and framing the things you see around you, as if composing "that perfect shot"?

◆ What do you think about sharing the images you capture?

◆ How could you see yourself integrating this practice in your life?

playing with my dolls

erik walker wikstrom

I know. A lot of people think it odd that a man in his fifties plays with dolls—even if he calls them "action figures." Nonetheless, I am unabashed in my enthusiasm for my hobby of collecting these flexible superhero dolls that can be posed in different ways. At the time of this writing, I have almost a hundred figures, the vast majority of which are different versions of Batman and his closest allies and villains. I keep a dozen or so in my office, along with my collection of Batmobiles, replicas of a batarang, Thor's hammer, and Captain America's shield. (I also have some more minister-like stuff in my office.)

I'm not just a collector, though. I don't keep my action figures behind glass—much less in their unopened boxes—and I don't require you to put on gloves so that you don't leave damaging oil behind if you're going to touch them. I play with my dolls. In odd moments, two of them might be engaged in a conversation or a battle or might just be flying around me while I try to get my imagination to take flight (when I'm writing a sermon, for example). Most often, though, my play consists of taking their pictures. I have an app on my phone and my iPad that allows me to use green-screen technology to create almost any backdrop I want—a nighttime roof, a dangerous alley, a sewer, a Japanese temple.

With other apps, I can add fog, explosions, or laser beams. When I'm done playing, I post the ones I like best to an album in my Flickr account.

I can easily get lost in one of these projects; there are so many different parts to it. I look for images online to use as backdrops and then try to select the right figure(s) to go with them. Even the figures with multiple points of articulation can be hard to pose, just from the sheer physics involved, yet getting a pose that tells a story is always a goal. Proper lighting is important so that the figure looks as if it belongs in the scene. Then there's all the postproduction work, from adjusting color saturation to adding special effects. Each piece of the process adds something to the mosaic of the whole, and each can be totally involving.

For about a year, I've been taking things up a notch. I now make three-dimensional backdrops, dioramas, or sets for the figures. I created a Batcave that, if made to scale, would be sixty-six feet long and twenty-four feet high, large enough for a meeting of the Justice League without anyone feeling crowded. I made a Batcomputer out of balsa wood, with monitor screens consisting of images taken from comics and the Internet placed behind Plexiglas. I designed it so that I can change the images, creating the potential for many different scenes with just this one prop.

While the big picture is important, the details make things pop. On the desk of that Batcomputer, there is a small framed photograph of his parents, Thomas and Martha Wayne, and a family portrait of Bruce and the various young men who have been Robin over the years. You might also see some wanted posters of well-known villains and one with tiny photographs of my sons.

Since superheroes have to stay in shape, I've also made props for a Bat-gym—a barbell from a thin dowel, some medicine bottle tops, parallel bars, a heavy punching bag, a pommel horse, and a wall of martial arts weapons (most of which

I simply repainted, but there's a homemade pair of 1/12-scale nunchucks I'm pretty proud of). I build these set and prop pieces in my garage workshop/photography studio. When I'm done, I select appropriate figures, pose them to suggest relationships and narrative, light the scene, and manipulate the image digitally.

Why do I think this is a spiritual practice? On the one hand, I could say that anything we do can be a spiritual practice if we intend it to be one. That's a bit of a cop-out, though, akin to saying that "everything is meditation." It's true to some degree, yet at least equally untrue. Another common name for spiritual practice is *spiritual discipline*, and the discipline dimension can easily get lost when we think that anything and everything we do is a practice. This sense of discipline—which we could also call "consistency," "commitment," or "accountability"—seems to be increasingly falling out of favor. I tell my children that when I was a kid, we had to wait an *entire week* to see what would happen next on a favorite TV show. And if you weren't there, right in front of your TV at the appointed time, you'd have to wait until the episode was rerun during the summer. There were no DVRs. Some things—like *The Grinch Who Stole Christmas* or *The Great Escape*—were annual events, and if you missed it during the one night it was on you'd have to wait a *whole year* for another chance. Today we can watch a favorite movie or TV special over and over again whenever we want, and an entire season (or two, or three) of a show over the course of a weekend. As a society, we're increasingly accustomed to getting things when we want, where we want, and how we want them. The commitment required for practicing a discipline appears to be less and less in demand.

I don't say, then, that my collecting and playing with my action figures is a spiritual practice because anything can be a spiritual practice. But it does have seven of the characteristics that all the great spiritual practices have in common.

It Requires Commitment

That pair of nunchucks didn't just appear one day, fully formed. I had to find a chain that was small enough and the right sized dowel for the figures' hands. Then I had to figure out how to attach that chain to the two pieces of dowel I'd cut. The painting itself was a multistep process, so that if you zoom in on the image it looks like real wood. None of this was easy, nor did any of it work out the first time I tried. Since hours of searching the Internet failed to yield any detailed plans for creating one-twelfth-scale nunchucks, I made it up as I went along. I was tempted to give up many times, but I didn't because I was committed to the overall project and recognized the importance of each step.

It Requires Regularity

While "the journey *is* the destination," getting somewhere can be awfully nice. With this practice, the "there" I'm aiming for is a finished photograph, one I consider good enough to put online and share. That means I need to keep at it. I can't take that picture until I finish work on the Batcomputer or finish the Batcomputer until I put the images behind the monitor screens, and I can't do that until I find the right images. Each step depends on the preceding ones and makes possible the ones that come after. If I don't keep up with it, the whole production grinds to a halt . . . and I take too much pleasure in it to let that happen.

It Has Interior Circularity

What I mean by "interior circularity" is that different aspects of the practice feed one another. Crafting a really cool set piece makes me want to take a photo, and each photo I take inspires me to want to create new and more detailed settings. In many well-recognized spiritual practices, an interior focus moves into outward action, which then turns the practitioner inward. This dimension of spiritual practice is often overlooked when all you do, for instance, is spend time in meditation or in community action work.

It Is Flexible

Sometimes I slip out into the workshop and give something a quick coat of paint when I'm already downstairs moving the laundry around. Other times, I turn off the ringer on my phone and settle in for a couple of hours of total immersion. Some practices demand a certain amount of time—thirty minutes in the morning and evening, for instance. However, practices that can fit into and around our already demanding schedules have a greater chance of taking root in our lives.

It Takes Me Away from My Daily Life

When I am in the workshop, carefully cutting, gluing, pasting, or adjusting a figure or the lighting so that a shadow enhances a scene, I am not thinking about the mundane minutiae that generally make up my inner monologue. I'm not ticking off items from my to-do list or thinking of things to add to it. I'm not replaying an argument from earlier in the day, nor am I preparing myself for one I expect to have that night. I'm not anywhere except where I am—at the workbench, playing with my dolls. As with so many spiritual practices, it draws me to a single point for a period of time, a major change from my usual state of scatteredness.

It Is Not Entirely Divorced from My Daily Life

I don't have to make an arduous climb to a mountaintop temple to engage in my practice. It's right there in the garage, attached to the laundry room of my house. I have carved out a portion of the space for my practice, but it is not in a different world. There is power in practices that require you to shave your head, put on special clothing, and go off to a distant place. But this practice *in* the world I inhabit everyday holds power for me. At the same time, my practice is integrated into my life in another way: I also collect comic books, watch superhero movies, and read blogs about them. My practice grows out of my love of superheroes, which are modern analogs for the mythological heroes and adventurers of old, as well as being the personification of the best (and worst) of humanity . . . with really cool powers. So my practice deepens and feeds what is already a part of my life.

It Brings Me Joy

Joy is, perhaps, a word that many people don't associate with the idea of spiritual practice. Yet even practices that involve austerities tend to open participants to experiences of great joy. For all the very real pain and hardship around (and within) us, we live in a miraculously beautiful world, and our opportunity to be a part of it is a great gift. Most spiritual practices, if fully understood and deeply engaged, make one aware and appreciative of that gift. I find this to be true of this practice as well.

Someone might say that everything I've written would apply to someone who collects stamps, for instance, or does scrapbooking. I don't disagree. I'm advocating for thinking about hobbies as spiritual practices. Is there something that you do, once did, or have thought about doing that has these seven characteristics? Congratulations! You may have identified a spiritual practice.

questions for your consideration

◆ What do you think of the seven characteristics of spiritual practice described in this chapter? Are there any you would add? Are there any that you think don't belong?

◆ Have you ever thought that a spiritual practice could be something others might consider frivolous or silly?

◆ Do you have a hobby that you've never before considered a spiritual practice? Are you seeing it in a new way now?

◆ Is there a hobby you used to engage in that you've now stopped doing? Why did you stop? What would you need to start doing it again?

roller derby

dawn skjei cooley

We are halfway into a two-hour practice and have just lined up to do a blocking drill with full contact. As my turn approaches, I breathe in and out. I envision where on the track I will catch up to my teammate and how I will angle my wheels to slide my hips in front of her, getting in the correct position to then drop low and thrust my shoulder into her chest to throw her backward. In my mind's eye, I am successful. When the whistle blows, I lay on the speed. I start breathing heavy, in and out.

Midway around the track, I catch my teammate, and as I go to slide in front of her, the top of our arms touch. Her skin is so slick that my shoulder slides in front of her fast enough to throw off my balance. Before I know it, I am face down, breathing in the stink of the floor. My teammate has leapt over me gracefully.

I get back up and go stand in line to wait my turn to try again. I try to catch my breath: breathe in. Breathe out. Breathe in. Breathe out.

Roller derby has been experiencing quite a rebirth. The sport began in the 1920s, when it was simply a race on four-wheel skates. Not until later did it begin to focus on skater collisions and falls. Before its current incarnation, roller derby hit its high point in the 1960s and 70s. During this period, the sport was much like pro wrestling—more about theatrics than athletic ability. In the early 2000s, roller derby was reborn in Austin, Texas. Today, athleticism has overtaken theatricality. Elbows to the face are not allowed, but elite skaters can perform stunts on their toe-stops that seem impossibly agile. Roller derby, primarily a sport participated in and run by women, appeals to people across ages, professions, and education levels.

I played for the Derby City Roller Girls in Louisville, Kentucky, for a few years under the name "Liv Fearless." Though I can't say I loved every minute of it, I did feel more grounded after practice sessions. Solutions to problems that had previously evaded me suddenly became clear, and I often left feeling like my best self. These qualities made me realize that roller derby had become more than a sport or hobby for me. I realized it had become a spiritual practice—something that, as Claudia Horwitz writes in *The Spiritual Activist: Practices to Transform Your Life, Your Work, and Your World*, is "simply a habit that gives us energy and reminds us of what matters most." She outlines three characteristics of a spiritual practice, and for me, roller derby hit every one.

The first characteristic of a spiritual practice, Horwitz writes, is that it "connects us to the presence of the sacred or that which has great meaning in our lives." As a mother and as a minister, I spend the majority of my time taking care of other people. My relationships to them matter, but I am able to feed those bonds daily—sometimes even to the point of forgetting to take care of myself. Playing roller derby helped me to remember the wisdom in what flight attendants say: to put on my *own* oxygen mask on before assisting others. Roller derby never failed to remind me of the importance of *me*.

My theology is built around my understanding of how precious and wonderful my life is and, at the same time, how minuscule I am in the vastness of the universe. Sri Nisargadatta Maharaj writes, "Wisdom is knowing I am nothing, Love is knowing I am everything, and between the two my life moves." Roller derby helped me move between these two. It got me into my body and reminded me that I am made from the stuff of the universe. Whether it was a bruise from a fall, the exhaustion of a well-spent practice, or the completion of a skill that I had been struggling to learn, I would leave each practice session with a deep gratitude for my health, for my life, and for the love and support of my family, who not only allowed but encouraged me to pursue my dreams.

The second characteristic of a spiritual practice, according to Horwitz, is that it "is something we do regularly (ideally on a daily basis) and without interruption." Though roller derby practices were usually only two or three times a week, with games—called *bouts*—only once or twice a week at most, I thought about the sport almost daily. I would think about the volunteer work I was doing for the team to help sustain it, or I would do a physical exercise that would help build my skating skills through cross-training. Roller derby was an integral part of my everyday life.

The third and final characteristic of a spiritual practice, says Horwitz, is that it "grounds us in the present moment, bringing us into awareness of what is happening right now." This awareness is a form of mindfulness and is often practiced through monitoring one's breath. Thich Nhat Hanh, famed Vietnamese Zen Buddhist monk, teacher, author, poet, and peace activist, writes in *You Are Here: Discovering the Magic of the Present Moment*, "As you breathe in, you can say to yourself, 'Breathing in, I know that I am breathing in.' When you do this, the energy of mindfulness embraces your in-breath, just like sunlight touching the leaves and branches of a tree. . . . As you breathe out, you can gently say, 'Breathing out, I know that I am breathing out.'"

While I am quite certain Hanh did not have roller derby skating drills in mind when he wrote about mindfulness, and while there was nothing gentle about the breathing I did, playing roller derby often had me more focused on the moment than any other time during the day. My mind, which is usually running ninety miles per hour, would stop thinking about my to-do list, my worry over my children, my hopes for the church I served. My mind would slow as I focused on my breath, my posture, my muscles, or the move I was about to execute. I would become grounded in the present moment.

Horwitz also says that "if the practice fills you with awe, at least most of the time, it will likely be something that can sustain and delight you, even when it is challenging." There were many times when derby was challenging—when I hurt too much to continue, when I didn't understand the complex rules, when I was frustrated in myself or a teammate. And yet this would pass. There was never a time when, even if I didn't feel like going, I regretted attending a practice session. I always felt better at the end.

As much as I loved it, though, I found it hard to return to the habit of attending roller derby practice sessions if I had to miss them for a prolonged time. When I least wanted to go, I usually most *needed* to. But it was sometimes difficult to overcome inertia. This is how it is with spiritual practices— they take discipline to *practice* them. And when we get out of the habit, it can kill our practice. When a family crisis caused me to miss derby practice for several months, I tried to return but was unable to get back into the routine. The downside of roller derby as a spiritual practice is that, instead of every day for a few minutes, it is a few hours a couple of times a week; it is easy to miss one week, then another, and then be unable to continue. I miss it and hope someday to return. Like many skaters I know, I've not found anything that can take its place.

Though I would guess Horwitz never thought about roller derby as a likely candidate for a spiritual practice, it met the three characteristics she proposed. Spiritual practices are usually thought of as something gentler, introspective, and, well, more spiritual. But after trying breathing meditations, walking meditations, yoga, prayer, *lectio divina*, poetry, and journaling, I've learned that if my body is not strenuously engaged, my mind and spirit won't be either. And I know I am not alone.

For too long, there has been a perceived division between the mind and the body. Though this dualism stretches back to the time of Plato, the version that has most strongly influenced modern thought comes from René Descartes, a French philosopher, scientist, and mathematician at the beginning of the Renaissance. He argued that the mind and the body are separate and therefore governed by different sets of laws. The body, he said, was like a machine and followed the laws of nature. The mind (or soul, as he called it) was not something physical and thus did not conform to the laws of nature. However, thoughts, Descartes argued, were governed instead by the rules of reasoning, judgment, and passions (what we now call emotions). Human beings are made up of a duality: physical bodies and immaterial minds.

Neeta Mehta, in her 2011 paper "Mind-Body Dualism: A Critique from a Health Perspective," writes that this separation of the mind and the body played a vital role in the development of the field of medicine in the seventeenth century. Orthodox Christianity viewed the body and the soul as one and believed that diseases of the body came from sinning against God. In order for the soul to ascend to heaven at death, the body had to be preserved intact. "As a result," Mehta observes, "there was a religious prohibition on the study of human anatomy through dissection. Descartes, through mind-body dualism, demythologised body and handed over its study to medicine." While this separation allowed enormous progress in medicine, it created a false dichotomy that denies the connection between the mind, spirit, self, and the body—a connection we know exists.

Today, although this dualistic understanding of human nature continues to undergird modern medicine, we see a bigger picture: What we do with our bodies affects not just our physical health but also our mental, emotional, and spiritual health. For example, exercise makes it easier for us to concentrate and raises levels of serotonin, leading to increased feelings of well-being. And it works the other way as well, with our mental and emotional status influencing our bodies. One example is how our bodies react to stress by releasing adrenaline and cortisol, causing heart rates to quicken and blood pressure to rise. Over time, too much exposure to stress can cause heart conditions, ulcers, and more. We now understand that our physical health, intellectual health, emotional health, and spiritual health are all connected.

Rinpoche Sakyong Mipham, a marathon-running Tibetan lama, in his book *Running with the Mind of Meditation: Lessons for Training Body and Mind*, writes:

> Because the mind and the body are intimately connected, relieving the stress of the body through exercise has an immediate effect on the mind. . . . It is not a matter of choosing what is better—exercising the mind or exercising the body. Rather, these activities go hand in hand. We need to exercise both our body and our mind. . . . When we give our mind and body what benefits them, a natural harmony and balance takes place. With this unified approach, we are happy, healthy and wise.

I experienced this reality when I played roller derby. My mind would consider the complex rules and strategies and what I needed my body to do. My body would move, test its limits, and stretch beyond what I thought I could do. Who knew I was able to blast full speed ahead and leap over a fallen skater in front of me, landing gracefully on the track and continuing my lap? Overcoming such challenges made me feel good about myself and my capabilities. Seeing the improvement I made was encouraging. And doing so with a host of other women, my teammates, warmed my heart. I was a part of something special.

Playing roller derby was fun. I would laugh, curse, and sweat. We wore crazy socks and tights under our safety pads. We made up secret identities for ourselves. We danced and laughed when standing in line, waiting for our turn in a drill. We played loud music. We called each other names and talked smack, always with a smile. Where else are you not only able, but encouraged, to hip-check someone so hard she lands on her butt? In an article for *Psychology Today*, "Playfulness Is a Spiritual Practice," Bernie De Koven writes, "Playfulness is a practice that shapes our souls. It connects us. It is an act of belief in ourselves, the vehicle whose wheels are powered by our faith in life, bringing us to places of wonder, moments of joy."

This was my experience with roller derby—a sport that started out as a way for me to make friends and engage my body and turned into an unlikely spiritual practice that engaged my entire being. Practiced regularly, it connected me mindfully with my body. It reminded me of my place in the universe and gave me space and time to breathe, to be myself. On top of that, it was fun. I still wear the tights.

questions for your consideration

◆ How did you *feel* when reading the author's experience of roller derby as a spiritual practice?

◆ Is there a practice you used to do that, for one reason or another, you are no longer able to do?

◆ The author says that if her body isn't "strenuously engaged" in her practice, then she knows her mind and spirit won't be either. Do you do anything now that engages your body in this way, and did you ever consider it a candidate for your spiritual practice?

◆ How might you integrate a practice like this into your own life?

practices born in daily life

the spiritual practice of chop, chop, chopping

linnea nelson

When I was a little girl, my Saturday morning chores included housecleaning, gardening, and baking. Baking was my joy, and I was known for making multiple batches of sweets every Saturday afternoon—chunky chocolate chip cookies, moist and spicy pumpkin bread, floury loaves of white bread, and our family's favorite: Swedish rolls drizzled with powdered sugar frosting and dusted with colored sprinkles to match the season.

I was so happy baking!

I believe that, in my childhood, my goal was to create and nurture joy—bite by bite. My mother helped by encouraging me and appreciating my efforts, as she seemed to feel that cooking and baking were tedious and time-consuming chores. I realize now that, in my childhood, I had developed the "regular practice" part of spiritual practices, but I didn't discover the "intentional practice" piece for quite some time. Especially as an adult, I got busier and busier and even the "regular" part faded away. I hired housecleaners (I'd done enough of that as a kid and would rather work longer at another job to pay for it) and ordered my groceries online, delivered by cheerful truck drivers who offered to line my countertops with colorful, crinkly, reusable bags of raisins, rice, and sugar next to various sizes of boxed cereal, cake mixes, and crackers. As I look back, I only see the overly packaged containers; the food was generally hidden by colorful advertising and words such as "new and improved." As I got busier with work, family, and volunteer commitments, we also started to order takeout food, eat at restaurants more frequently, and depend on big-box stores that sold huge quantities of frozen and processed foods that were easy to throw together and call a meal. I was completely disconnected from the food I was using to fuel myself and my family.

Luckily, my career moved from school administrator to religious educator. One of the joys of being a religious educator is that I often stumble upon new and meaningful ways to live my life as part of my day-to-day job. A transformation came when I participated in a year-long class that required members to explore and share a variety of spiritual practices. I was fascinated by the array of ways people chose to center themselves. I heard about meditation with spa-like music softly playing in the background; walking slowly with deliberate steps; sitting in silence and in groups; spreading watercolor paint across blank paper with abandon; using black-and-white line drawings for meditative coloring; books of delicious poetry; bound journals sprinkled with inspirational quotes; and the gentle and gracious movements of tai chi chih. All these practices introduced me to how it feels to slow down and pay attention. I was learning to be intentional about the smallest of movements and actions and to appreciate the way I was feeling in any given moment. I was beginning to find out who I was deep inside.

Slowly, I started being okay with doing something that was not overly productive or based on using all of my intellectual skills at the highest level, which in the past usually included ignoring my body, my soul, and my senses. As I explored each of these spiritual practices, I came to realize that I was hurrying through everything—the painful and distasteful as well as the joyful and comforting moments in life. I seemed to never relax into the moment and reflect on how my body or spirit was reacting to and engaging with the world.

Meditation helped me slow down, but my love of cooking brought me back to my heart. My spiritual home must actually be somewhere baked into my kitchen. Here, as an adult, I unexpectedly discovered the power of mindful vegetable chopping.

As a child, I was into sugar and flour and decorating. Vegetable chopping seemed incredibly boring to me. But all of a sudden, a butcher knife stopped being just a dusty tool in my drawer. I could feel its handle and shiny, wide blade as my hand guided the knife to puncture the celery and land with a thud on the cutting board. I bought brand-new smooth bamboo cutting boards, a sharpening stone, and glass bowls with lids to properly store the vegetables, which were like colorful gems. I became entranced by familiar but unexamined tools: a fancy new peeler that fit on my middle finger and allowed my whole hand to graze a potato or peel an eggplant. Metal waves along a forgotten chopper made ribbed coins out of bright orange—or sometimes purple or yellow—heirloom carrots. New hand tools made springy spirals out of zucchini and ribbons of fresh red beets. And the joy of rinsing the vegetables in cold, cold running water would lead me to do an extra wash as dust dissolved and the color emerged, shiny in my hand. I would open the tap to run water around and over and through the broccoli crowns, inside the cut red peppers to rinse away the seeds, and over the torn leaves of lettuce or spinach. But my favorite thing was to unwrap a big, white, beautiful head of cauliflower.

When I shared my newfound chopping spiritual practice with my class, I gave each of them a large kale leaf, drizzled with olive oil and a sprinkle of sea salt. I taught them to massage the leaf and to really feel the wonder of this ridiculously healthy food, grown organically, and now serving as a gift to each of us. We commented on the dark-green color, the deep nourishment it provided, and the gratitude we had for the people who worked in the fields to cultivate this beautiful plant. We tore the leaves into small pieces; some brave class members ate their own massaged leaf while remarking that this was indeed a very unique spiritual practice. They still tease me occasionally in good fun.

As this regular and intentional spiritual practice became an important part of my life, I sought out sources of unique and organic vegetables and kept my knives sharpened. I joined a Community Supported Agriculture (CSA) cooperative and found freshly picked vegetables on my doorstep every Friday morning. I began listening to inspiring podcasts while creating recipes based on these mystery bags of fresh and local vegetables each week. I bought a juicer, a dehydrator, and then a Vitamix to process all the vegetables I was chopping and chopping and chopping. I doused green smoothies, cauliflower soup, bean dips, and spinach puree with my personalized savory treatments that began in recipe books and ended with a pinch of cumin or a handful of parsley. But the key for me is that each dish begins with a *chop* of my knife through a crisp vegetable.

One of my favorite parts of returning from a vacation is pulling open the refrigerator doors and checking for any rogue vegetables that are now limp or shriveled. No matter the condition, I often carefully clean and chop them. If I can use them, fine, but if they are too far gone, my carefully chopped cubes of mushy zucchini or strips of browning spinach might go straight to compost. My need to feel the skin of each vegetable, to feel the resistance of the knife against the flesh, and to see the inside of each vegetable where the seeds or stalks lie has become my spiritual practice. Eating it has become secondary.

My childhood practice of baking *seemed* to be about nurturing my family and the friends who frequently dropped by our house or business. But now I realize that it was more about the repetitive—some might say boring—nature of stirring and measuring. This has morphed into the chop, chop, chopping that seems to bring me inner peace and a sense of being enough to just be chopping vegetables. I've found each chop brings me closer to eating mindfully and taking better care of our planet.

The rhythmic chop, chop, chopping and the deep understanding that I am using these vegetables to connect my body and spirit to the natural world brings me great peace. Mindfully chopping vegetables to feed myself and my family helps me feel and give love. The practice also deepens my appreciation for the earth and connects me to the people who toil to grow and provide the parade of colorful vegetables to my home, galvanizing my spiritual self every single day.

questions for your consideration

♦ The Buddhist monk Thich Nhat Hanh teaches about "washing dishes meditation," and the Christian mystic Brother Lawrence says his work in the monastery kitchen is a form of prayer. How do you experience daily household tasks?

♦ Were you surprised to read that the author considers the chopping, in and of itself, to be the practice, more than the total preparation of the meal? Is there a piece of a larger activity that speaks to you?

♦ How might you integrate a practice like this into your own life?

the bloom of the present moment

barry andrews

I once believed that religion was primarily a matter of scriptures, creeds, and rituals. But over the years, I have changed my mind about the nature and object of religion. Religion is not so much about believing as it is about living. It is not so much about meaning as it is about passion. It is not so much about doctrines as it is about waking up, about being fully alive in the awareness of the present moment. I agree with a remark by Ralph Waldo Emerson in his journal. Religion, he writes, "is not something else *to be got*, to be *added*, but is a new life of those faculties you have." It is neither beliefs nor rituals. It is life.

For me, the essence of religion is waking up, becoming alive. When I was a child, I used to say the familiar prayer: "Now I lay me down to sleep. I pray the Lord my soul to keep. If I should die before I wake, I pray the Lord my soul to take." Today my prayer is simply to wake up before I die. Most of the time, it appears to me as though we are sleepwalking through life. Anesthetized, distracted, dulled to joy and pain alike, we become mired in everyday routine. Whole chunks of our lives go by in a flash. When did my children get so big? Where did all these wrinkles and gray hairs come from? How did I get to where I am today?

My reading of the Transcendentalists has led me to the insistence that every moment is precious and we must make the most of each one, that the greatest challenge of life is to wake up before we die, and that this is what religion is really all about. In his poem "Days," Emerson writes that the days of our lives offer us gifts that we may either accept or refuse. Forgetting his "morning wishes"—that is to say, his youthful aspirations—Emerson hastily takes only "a few herbs and apples." Too late does he realize the lost opportunity—he let pass unclaimed the many wonders of "Bread, kingdoms, stars, and sky that holds them all" that he was offered and says that the day "Turned and departed silent." The same is often true for us. Every day offers us gifts that we are too busy or too distracted to appreciate.

No one was more insistent on this score than Henry David Thoreau. In 1845, he went to Walden Pond to contemplate the purpose of life. He wrote *Walden*, he said, in an effort to wake up his neighbors. "Why is it that human beings give so poor an account of their day if they have not been slumbering?" he asks. He knew—as we should also know—that only in the present moment can there be happiness or change or growth. Life exists only in the here and now. "We are always getting ready to live," Emerson said. There is "very little life in a lifetime." Only by making the most of every moment can we be assured of living life to its fullest. This may seem obvious or even superficial. When you're young and you seem to have your whole life in front of you, you think you have plenty of time to spare. As we get older, however, there is a poignant urgency to savor experience as fully as possible.

As with so many things, this is easier said than done. Awareness is the key, obviously. The best way—indeed, the only way—to capture moments is to pay attention. Attentiveness means waking up. Although this may seem simple, it is not necessarily easy. Our habitual lack of awareness, our tendency to be distracted and dissatisfied, keeps us benumbed.

To wake up, to achieve awareness, requires intentionality and it takes practice. It is how we cultivate our souls. As an everyday spiritual exercise, I try to do what Thoreau suggests: "I got up early and bathed in the pond; that was a religious exercise, and one of the best things which I did." I don't have a pond nearby to take a dip in, but I do find it invigorating to stretch my legs, to get up and get moving, early in the morning. Not only do I shake off slumber, but I also feel that the day is longer and richer with possibilities. As Thoreau so memorably put it, "Only that day dawns to which we are awake."

Becoming aware means being present in the moment. We are not trying to improve ourselves or to get somewhere else. We can do this in any place at any time, taking each moment as it comes. Thoreau went to Walden Pond to cultivate attentiveness, but the universe coalesces at every point in space and time, such that any moment and any place can be a gateway to the infinite. "God himself culminates in the present moment," Thoreau writes, "and will never be more divine in the lapse of all the ages. And we are enabled to apprehend at all what is sublime and noble only by the perpetual instilling and drenching of the reality that surrounds us." I find that wherever I am, even in the midst of the city, I am able to catch glimpses of the sublime if I take the time to slow down and look around.

While living at the pond, Thoreau would often sit in his doorway for hours and simply watch and listen as the sun moved across the sky and the light and shadows changed almost imperceptibly. He says:

There were times when I could not afford to sacrifice the bloom of the present moment to any work, whether of the head or hands. . . . I grew in those seasons like corn in the night, and they were far better than any work of the hands would have been. They were not time subtracted from my life, but so much over and above my usual allowance. I realized what the Orientals [sic] mean by contemplation and the forsaking of works.

Contemplation is an important part of my own spiritual practice. I hesitate to call it meditation because it does not involve formal exercises of body, breathing, or brain. It is a relaxed awareness. Behind my home, I have a small Chinese-style garden, where, in one secluded corner, weather permitting, I sit in a chair as Thoreau did in his sunny doorway. The hours I linger there are measured by the movement of the sun, not the hands of a clock. I listen to the birds and watch them bathe in the nearby birdbath. I muse and daydream, read and write. The news and social media are strictly off limits. Although I do not think of this practice in practical terms, it is the most productive and well-spent period of my day.

Like Thoreau, we should savor the moment-to-moment unfolding of the present. We are so busy hurrying about, trying to get ahead of the person in the lane next to us, that one day we will discover that we have simply rushed through life and now it is gone. In his book *Wherever You Go, There You Are*, Jon Kabat-Zinn writes, "Who is to say that [Thoreau's] realizations of one morning spent in his doorway are less memorable or have less merit than a lifetime of busyness, lived with scant appreciation for stillness and the bloom of the present moment?" Thoreau was teaching a lesson as important today as in his own time, pointing out the importance of contemplation and detachment.

In keeping with Thoreau's insistence that "We must learn to reawaken and keep ourselves awake," the Transcendentalists engaged in a number of spiritual practices aimed at achieving this result. These were part and parcel of what they called "self-culture." While the term sounds a little quaint to the modern ear, it means, quite simply, the cultivation of the soul. Their practice—which I have long since adopted in a modest way as my own—consisted of walks in nature, contemplation, solitude, reading, journal writing, deep conversations with friends, and simple living. The Transcendentalists held that spirituality required an outward manifestation of inward aspirations. For them, the moral and the spiritual were necessarily interrelated. Accordingly, they sought to achieve congruence between spiritual insights and ethical actions in all areas of their lives.

Here on Bainbridge Island where I live, I love to go for walks in the Grand Forest, at Bloedel Gardens, or along the beach, all within easy reach. *Sauntering* was the term Thoreau gave to walking as a spiritual discipline. He took notes of his thoughts and observations as he walked, but he viewed his walks as a form of meditation: "I think that I cannot preserve my health and spirits, unless I spend four hours a day at least—and it is commonly more than that—sauntering through the woods and over the hills and fields, absolutely free from all worldly engagements." A few hours in the course of a busy week are all I am able to manage, but they are hours well spent. Whether in solitude or with friends, I enjoy sauntering in communion with nature, which uplifts my spirits and reminds me that I am part of something much larger than myself. For a few hours at least, I feel "free from all worldly engagements."

Reading was another important spiritual practice of the Transcendentalists. "To read well, that is, to read true books in a true spirit," Thoreau writes, "is a noble exercise, and one that will task the reader more than any exercise which the customs of the day esteem." They read the classics, poetry, and scriptures of other religions, seeking inspiration rather than information. My reading, too, has consisted largely of poetry and the spiritual classics. Rumi, Wordsworth, Whitman, and Mary Oliver are my favorite poets. I include the *Meditations* of Marcus Aurelius, the *Bhagavad Gita*, the *Dhammapada*, the *Tao Te Ching*, the *Analects* of Confucius, the writings of Mencius and Chuang-tzu, *Walden*, and Emerson's essays in my library of spiritual classics. Contemporary writers, especially Annie Dillard, Thomas Moore, Parker Palmer, and Jack Kornfield, also remind me of the wisdom to be gained from reading as a spiritual practice.

Many religious liberals have expressed a desire for more spiritual depth in their lives and their churches. They have found spiritual richness in Buddhism, Judaism, Christianity, goddess religion, paganism, and other religious faiths. I have discovered it in my own tradition. As historian David Robinson observes,

> Like a pauper who searches for the next meal, never knowing of the relatives whose will would make him rich, American Unitarians lament their vague religious identity, standing upon the richest theological legacy of any American denomination. Possessed of a deep and sustaining history of spiritual achievement and philosophical speculation, religious liberals have been, ironically, dispossessed of that heritage.

The heritage he refers to is that of Transcendentalism. In my writing and my own everyday spiritual practice, I have tried to reclaim that heritage.

More than anything else, the Transcendentalists—Emerson and Thoreau, in particular—have instructed me in the art of life. In his journal, the intimate record of his inner life, Thoreau reflects,

> The art of life! Was there ever anything memorable written upon it? By what disciplines to secure the most life, with what care to watch our thoughts. To observe what transpires, not in the street, but in the mind and heart of me! I do not remember any page

which will tell me how to spend this afternoon. . . .
The art of spending a day. If it is possible that we
may be addressed, it behooves us to be attentive. If by
watching all day and all night I may detect some trace
of the Ineffable, then will it not be worth the while to
watch?

In my own way, I have attempted to adopt the disciplines
they developed for securing what Thoreau called "the most
life." Through contemplation and solitude, reading and conversations with friends, walks in nature and modest living,
I find myself better able to "observe what transpires, not in
the street, but in the mind and heart of me." Occasionally, I
have detected traces of the ineffable. And that has made all
the difference.

questions for your consideration

◆   Do you have any time in your day (week, month, year) when you are truly "free from all worldly engagements"? If not, can you think why not and how you can create such time?

◆   Do you have a quiet place like the author's small garden or Thoreau's doorway?

◆   How often do you get to "saunter" in nature? For that matter, how often do you "saunter" anywhere? What does that word call to mind for you?

◆   Do you read any books for spiritual practice?

the whole of the spiritual life: a meditation on friendship

james ishmael ford

> One day while walking quietly together, out of the silence the Buddha's attendant Ananda declared, "Teacher, to have companions and comrades on the great way is so amazing! I have come to realize that friendship is fully half of an authentic spiritual life." They proceeded along quietly for a while more, before out of that silence the Holy One responded. "No, dear one. Without companions and comrades, no one can live into the deep, finding the true harmonies of life, to achieve authentic wisdom. To say it simply, friendship is the whole of the spiritual life."
>
> —Upaddha Sutta, freely adapted

It's been a number of years, but I remember the email clearly. It was from a member of the congregation I was serving in Massachusetts. She invited me to become her Facebook friend. While I'd never before that moment given any thought to joining a web-based social network, this invitation was so sweet. I couldn't recall the last time someone asked me to be a friend.

I followed the link she provided and filled out the required form. However, as I came to the part that asked if I would like to invite my email address book to be Facebook friends, before I actually had finished reading the question and absorbing its meaning, I had already pushed the yes button. Almost instantly I had nearly four hundred friends. Today, that number is more than four thousand.

Another aspect of my electronic life was the various email lists to which I belonged—some were official, most were not. Among these were several for Unitarian Universalist ministers. I never followed any of them closely.

I used to advise seminarians to join the official clergy email list as soon as they were able—if for no other reason than by reading it, the seminarians would be assured that if some of the people posting to the list could be ministers, then they could too. Of course, not everything the ministers posted was a waste of time.

Sometimes we would return repeatedly to a subject according to some mysterious rhythm, probably related to the alignment of the stars. Among these regular subjects were flurries of queries and responses about whether ministers should accept Facebook "friending" requests. And should they defriend congregants when they leave a congregation? The concern was that, in seminary, they'd all been told that there are two opinions about whether a minister can have friends within the congregation they serve.

The majority opinion is that ministers may not have friends in their congregation. The minority opinion is that it is excruciatingly difficult. These writers, not all brand-new ministers, worried that becoming Facebook friends would or could compromise their ministries. And that remaining friends after leaving a congregation would compromise their successor's ministry.

So, who might be a friend? A dear friend once gave me a good working definition of friendship. He said a friend is someone who will help you move. Having a somewhat jaundiced nature, he added that a real friend will help you move a body. I suggested that, as sweet as the Facebook term "friend" is, no one should assume a Facebook friend will ever help you move, either furniture or body. It's all pretty lightweight stuff. Or it is to all but the most naïve. So to my minister colleagues worried about friending or defriending on Facebook, I have always suggested: Get a grip. And maybe try to get some perspective.

Friendship is something that, I suspect, is more complicated than helping us move. Friendship is a mutable term with casual and more profound meanings. But I suggest that friendship is a part of that larger whole we call love.

Friendship and love are deeply connected. The Greeks, as anyone who has studied the New Testament knows, had four terms for aspects of what we call *love*. The big ones are *eros*, romantic or erotic love, and *agape*, what we usually think of as divine love. Given less attention, but nonetheless in the family of love are *storge*, affection or familial love, and *philia*, or friendship.

The Christian apologist C. S. Lewis wrote a delightful, if occasionally eccentric, study of these titled *The Four Loves*. He says that the loves inform each other. As we look at one kind of love, each of the others is illuminated and illuminates the whole of the dynamic human experience of intimacy.

I'm confident that this is what the Buddha meant when he told Ananda that friendship is "the whole of the spiritual life." As we explore each aspect of our intimate encounters, we're on the way to finding meaning and purpose and direction. We are on the way to genuine wisdom.

I think my role as an ordained clergyperson can serve as an example of the difficulties in understanding friendship, having friends, and being a friend. The relationship between parish ministers and the people in the congregation they serve presents somewhat unique challenges. We can't be identified

with a particular set or clique, and this makes it difficult to
pal around, to spend a lot of social time with any particular group of people. But really the challenge of developing
and maintaining friendships as a parish minister is most of
all about time.

Now retired from parish ministry, I still vividly recall my
guilty feelings when my wife Jan and I took a weekend away.
Over the years, whenever we went away, I would feel as if
I were stealing time from work that I must do. Throughout
my ministerial life, I never took all the vacation time I was
entitled to.

That difficulty acknowledged the kind of person I would
become if I didn't find time for friendship. What kind of person would I be if I didn't hazard the dangers of trying to be
friendly within the community, the place I live, and carve out
a little time and have some friendships?

Almost all of us are busy beyond reason. But what kind
of people are any of us going to be if we don't hazard the dangers, carve out some time, and try to have and be a friend?
Most of the people who come to a faith community do so
because of some pressing spiritual question. They are there
in quest of a spiritual life, a life with meaning and purpose.

The Buddha tells us that friendship is the whole of the
spiritual life. The Buddha was right.

Dividing the four loves helps us get some perspective on
the dynamic. So, agape—divine love—or our individual experience of the whole can't be understood without experiencing
each of the other three, to some degree. Here we find how all
the loves inform one another. For example, erotic love without a sense of affection inevitably becomes abusive. Familial
love that doesn't extend beyond the boundaries of the house
is narrow and tribal. And sadly, we know what evils follow
narrow, tribal loves.

Any friendship that isn't informed by all the dynamic variations of affection misses its real value. Divine love informs

erotic love, which informs affection, which informs friendship, which informs all the others. We live in a multicausal universe, and nowhere is this truth more obviously true than in how we engage and must engage our friendships.

Our friendships are that important and that complicated. In the spiritual life nowhere do our ideals meet the actual more obviously than in how we relate to each other, in how we make, sustain, and are friends.

So, what does this look like in real life? How are we friends? Friendship has many faces; it's complex. There are no real instructions for how to be a friend. Boundaries and abandon are part of it. Getting the right balance is hard. I've experienced getting it wrong a lot. But to have a worthwhile life, we must engage in the dance, even if we step on a toe now and again or have our own foot trod on. We learn by doing.

questions for your consideration

◆　If, as Buddha tells us, friendship is the whole of the spiritual life, what constitutes a friend? Are friends on Facebook or other social media "real" friends, or do friends need to be in more direct relationship?

◆　What drew you to your friends, and what do you think has drawn them to you?

◆　Do you have time to nurture your friendships and create new ones? If not, do you need to reconsider how you spend your time?

◆　How do you go about cultivating friendships—deepening the ones you already have or developing new ones? What has worked—and what has not worked—in the past? What might you do now?

on the days i eat

colleen mcdonald

When I am filled with uncontainable joy, I laugh. It happens sometimes when I am listening to classical music, and the piece is like an old friend I'd almost forgotten, until we meet again by surprise, and I discover she is even more delightful than I remembered.

When I was in my early forties, a piece of music on the radio changed my life. I don't recall what it was, or whether I laughed when I heard it. But I do remember vividly that I was driving to work and listening to the music so intently that I don't know how I stayed on the road. When it was over and I returned to earth, I thought, "In my next life, I'd like to play a musical instrument." Almost immediately, a second thought occurred: "What about *this* life?"

Among those of us who were offered music lessons in childhood but who quit our instrument before we were grown, I count myself among the 99.9 percent of adults who regret it. In my case, the instrument was the piano. My mother played the piano—though she rarely had the time— and I started lessons when I was in fifth grade. My memories of my studies are vague, though not unpleasant; there was no pressure, and no recitals, and I don't think I minded practicing. But two years after I began, I graduated into junior high and a world of extracurricular activities. For better or worse, my parents let me decide that I wasn't interested enough in piano to continue.

Still, I did love good music, and that passion stayed with me as I went to the symphony with my parents, sang in school choirs, amassed a record collection (in the days when music was captured on vinyl discs), and went to concerts and opera performances as an adult. Yet it wasn't until that spring day when the car radio was cranked up, and my ears were open wide enough to hear the sound of my own longing, that it dawned on me that my days as a pianist did not have to be over.

It took longer than I had expected to find a teacher, and when I did, she was about to take her summer break. Undeterred, I dug up a couple of piano books I'd held onto since elementary school and got permission to use my church's piano so I could start practicing again. Sixteen years later, I am still at it.

You only need to practice on the days you eat. That's the philosophy of the music school where I take my lessons. It means I sit down at the bench even on the days when I am tired or not in the mood, my throat is scratchy and I think I may be getting sick, I'm busy and preoccupied, or I am utterly frustrated by my lack of progress on the piece or skill at hand. I challenge myself to focus only on the music and the music making, and work at something that is hard for me, doing it over and over again until it becomes easier and more effective or expressive. It's no wonder many children need to be cajoled, pushed, or bribed into learning an instrument, and few adult students sustain their initial enthusiasm over the long haul.

What about this discipline is spiritual?

My piano, though a modest one, cost more money than most people will make in their lifetimes. The room where I practice is larger and more comfortable than many people's living space. Practicing reminds me that I am fortunate to have a job and money in the bank and that I live my life on

the top rung of Maslow's hierarchy of needs. While much
of the world's population struggles daily for survival, I have
time and resources to devote to music.

Despite all they have done for me all my life, my hands
are also something I took for granted before I returned to the
piano. When I look at them each day, I am reminded that
the human hand is a marvelous piece of work, giving us the
strength, sensitivity, precision, and control that allow us not
only to play instruments but to perform a much greater variety of manual tasks than any other animal on earth. At the
least, I am more careful and attentive when I chop vegetables
these days.

Learning and playing music is a call to mindfulness. Tin-
kering away until the timer goes off does not qualify as practicing, any more than sitting in lotus position and waiting
for the chimes to release you constitute meditating. Playing
music does not belong on a to-do list. Getting to the end and
finishing, or even playing all the notes in a piece correctly, is
not the point (though developing precision *is* a step along the
way). Composers mean to transport us—take us on a journey
—kindle our imagination, inspire hope and reverence, and
bring us solace and joy. Musicians strive to convey beauty,
excitement, and meaning; to communicate truth that cannot
be put into words; to create something intangible yet vibrant
and real, just short of birthing a living being. You cannot be
unconscious to enter into all that.

When I sit down to practice, I am usually thinking about
something other than piano, or looking ahead to the pieces
I am working on and planning what I want to accomplish
during the session. I need discipline to remember to center
myself in joy and gratitude and to set aside agendas and
stresses of the day; to sit up straight and take some cleansing
breaths; to be aware of tension in my body and consciously
relax; and to focus on bringing my body, mind, emotions,
and spirit into harmony in the service of making music.

Everyone wants to be able to just sit down and play. When learning music, you need to train yourself to be patient and to go slowly, moving at a snail's pace, phrase by phrase, chord by chord, note by note. (One of my teachers calls this "Zen practicing.") It takes far less energy to muddle through a piece while operating on automatic pilot. However, by lingering, we give ourselves time to notice where each note has come from and where it is going. This awareness helps our understanding and accuracy so we can pick up on details that make the music more interesting and expressive and ease into the motor patterns so that they eventually become more fluid. We do not gobble the music down. We learn to savor each bite.

Being in the moment with the music also means listening attentively, which is harder than you might think when your mind is occupied with notes and rhythms, technique and interpretation. It is natural to hear the clinkers that signal obvious mistakes. Musicians must tune in more deeply, listening for the quality of the sound or tone, the balance (or sometimes the parity) between the two hands, the clarity of the pedaling, the duration and volume of the notes, and even the silences, which can be drowned out without careful attention to the rests.

Playing the piano requires fine motor control of the fingers and bilateral coordination of the upper extremities. (Add the foot, when you are pedaling.) The cognitive aspect includes reading music—encompassing not only the ability to understand what is printed on the page but to discern what is not explicit but implied or assumed—and memorization. There are also creative and artistic dimensions that are grasped more by intuition than instruction. Good musicians enliven their repertoire by conjuring up images, even creating stories, that direct their musical interpretation. They infuse the music with personal meaning, bringing their heart and soul into their performances. Their music speaks for them, carrying a unique message as well as conveying the universal experience of being human.

To me, the level of skill that produces a virtuoso performance is nothing short of miraculous.

Pablo Casals, a world-renowned cellist, was ninety-three years old when someone asked him why he continued to practice three hours every day. Casals explained, "I'm beginning to notice some improvement." Music making teaches humility: Even after a lifetime of practice and study, there is always more to learn.

I participate in student recitals now. Among the pianists I join in these performances are children who are progressing faster than I am and who already play better than I ever will. Young musicians, who are able to think of the sky as their limit, have their whole lives ahead of them to learn and to grow into their musicianship. As an adult, I recognize I only have so much time and only so much talent. Playing the piano is much more difficult than I remembered or imagined. I give careful thought to the pieces I choose for serious study, knowing I can tackle only a few each year. There are many pieces I love and have dreamed about playing that are beyond me; sometimes I have to let go of old goals and set new ones.

It is tempting to fantasize about the music I might be able to play by now if I had stayed the course in seventh grade. But the discipline of musical performance teaches me not to be derailed, defeated, or defined by lapses and mistakes but, rather, to keep going. We can learn from the past, but we cannot change it; our power lies in giving our best to what lies in front of us right now.

I didn't have the dedication, determination, and desire, as a child, that I do as an adult. Perhaps now is the time I am meant to be at the piano. So, every day (almost!) I am back on the bench, yearning and striving for that transcendent moment when I am confident, prepared, at ease, and utterly focused, when I can just "sit down and play," and the instrument becomes my voice, and the music becomes *my* song.

I don't know about the next life. For now, I am grateful for the privilege and the pleasure of making music in *this* life. Sometimes, when I'm relaxed and in the moment, and the music has just flowed out of me, I lift my hands off the keyboard and I laugh.

questions for your consideration

- What role has music, or music making, played in your life? Have you had any spiritual experiences connected with music? If so, what made you think of it that way?

- In the daily routine of your life, what activities are as important to you as eating? Why are they so central?

- What does the phrase "only on the days you eat" mean to you? What would it be like for you to have that kind of commitment to a spiritual practice?

walking as a spiritual discipline

jonalu johnstone

When I took a sabbatical in 2011, I wanted to find a major endeavor that would connect with me spiritually and that would include my partner, Jane. She's a long distance back-packer who has completed three trails of more than two thousand miles in the United States—the Appalachian Trail, the Pacific Crest Trail, and the Continental Divide Trail. Though she doesn't define herself as a spiritual person, she has found that long distance trails ground her in a routine, and the trees sometimes open up and talk with her. The perfect way to bring together my interest in spirituality and her commitment to long walks was to undertake a pilgrimage—we'd walk the Camino de Santiago.

The Camino has served as a pilgrimage route since the Middle Ages, bringing seekers to the city of Santiago in Spain. For some time, it had faded into memory, with few pilgrims following its route. But in the past few decades—spurred by books by Paulo Coelho, Shirley MacLaine, and others, and recently by the movie *The Way*—the Camino has come back, drawing Italians and Germans, Koreans and Poles, and even a few Americans. With guidance from a British friend who had walked the Camino, we decided on the most popular route, the Camino Frances, five hundred miles from St. Jean Pied de Port in the French Pyrenees across the north of Spain to Santiago. In preparation, I immersed myself in the literature of pilgrimage and Santiago, and together Jane and I hiked to build up our tolerance for ten- to fifteen-mile days of backpacking, one day after another.

But nothing fully prepares you for the experience. "Buen Camino," says each pilgrim who meets or passes you, no matter their native language or background. The words, meaning more or less "Have a good walk," serve as a greeting, an acknowledgment, or a farewell, and mean more than words can really say. They mean, "I am with you on your journey," "Blessings," and "Hang in there." An international community of pilgrims grows up. You recognize people and learn a piece of their story. Maybe you never see them again, or you meet like old friends a week or two later.

Each day brings a new adventure. You read the guidebook but never really know what to expect. A town may loom ahead for hours as you trudge toward it, frustrated that you haven't reached it yet. Or you may suddenly turn a corner and find a village before you. You may travel alongside olive groves or eucalyptus forests, luxuriating in nature, or beside a crowded highway dangerously close to traffic.

You walk. For hours. Every day. You notice if you're hungry or thirsty or need a bathroom break. Meeting basic needs can require more planning and energy than you're used to. You fill your water bottle each time you pass a town fountain. You may pause for a coffee in mid-morning. Each afternoon, you stop at an albergue, a Spanish hostel for pilgrims, and follow your routine. Showering, washing clothes, resting your feet and treating your blisters, having dinner. Yet each place is different. In a rural area, dinner may be a shared pilgrims' meal at the albergue. You may seek out a restaurant or bar for a regional specialty—paella or Castilian garlic soup or tortilla (a frittata-like dish with potatoes). Or you may find a kitchen in the albergue, so you can pick something up in a nearby shop and cook your own meal. You'll probably have a glass of red wine, Rioja or Tempranillo, whatever the region specializes in. Wherever you are, you are a stranger, but you have a place, a role. You are a pilgrim (*peregrino/a*), and natives and pilgrims alike recognize you as such.

Layers of culture and history include ancient ruins from medieval pilgrimage sites and contemporary grand cathedrals, as well as tiny village churches with stunning portraits of disciples and saints. After hours of walking through the landscape each day, from time to time, awareness dawns that devout seekers have walked these paths for hundreds of years. As a pilgrim, your *credencial del peregrino*, the paper you carry carefully to document the places you've been, is stamped at each hostel or refuge where you take shelter and some churches and bars along the way. In Santiago, you'll present the credencial to receive the certificate showing that you completed the Camino.

The journey is social, historical, cultural, and physical. What makes the pilgrimage spiritual? For many pilgrims, it's the practices they do—attending mass, carrying a rock to add to the pile at the *Cruz de Ferro* (iron cross) and contemplating its special meaning for them, crafting crosses from sticks, or praying without ceasing. For me, it was the centering, what I came to call "Camino mind."

Camino mind is that state in which I walk tuned into my surroundings and open to what may come. I became radically aware of the unpredictability not only of the pilgrimage but also of life. Each day brings gifts that we cannot imagine before they come—the burst of red dots across a field of poppies, the rich nutty taste of sheep cheese, a surprising connection with a new companion, a stolen moment of rest and quiet in the pew of an empty church. Each day also brings challenges—a storm whose waters seep into your pack and through the clothes you're wearing, swollen feet or painful arches, a missed turn that leaves you wandering and adding useless miles, a full albergue and nowhere to sleep unless you walk on. We don't know what's around the corner or what's in store today. We can't plan for each event that may happen. We can only bring our full selves to what happens, rejoice in gratitude for the gifts, and rise to the challenges.

There's a saying about the Camino. In Spanish, the verb *hacer* can mean either "make" or "do." The saying is that you don't do the Camino; the Camino does you. Or you don't make the Camino; the Camino makes you. That, for me, is the spiritual message of the Camino. We are made by the way that we go, shaped by the experiences we have.

And since I have walked the Camino, that experience goes into the walking I do every day, and even into the way I live my life.

Getting Physical

Chances are no one would have pegged me as a kinesthetic learner when I was a child. I was clumsy and slow, an introverted reader playing more in my imagination than running around the yard. Yet, as I trained to be a teacher, I learned about different modalities of learning and grew to understand how my kinesthetic learning showed up. I'd take notes, not for the notes themselves but because the movement to form letters helped me remember what I had written, even if I never looked at the notes again. When challenged by a physical task, the movement often overflowed to my mouth, where my tongue would shift around as if to help in the physical demand.

Years later, I realized that, for me, the way to the spiritual was also through the physical. Time at the gym calmed and centered me. The discipline of tai chi taught me how to meditate. And the greatest and most versatile tool of all? A simple walk.

Like any spiritual discipline, it's not for everyone. Some people find it boring or too strenuous, but walking has always helped me. As an adolescent, I'd retreat to the woods around my house and meander when I felt stressed. More than once, I walked the four miles to high school. My dog allowed me plenty of chances to walk (or run) when I was a young adult. My partner and I even have a motto we share, "You can always walk another mile." It isn't always true, but it keeps us going, if not physically, at least spiritually.

Walking as a spiritual discipline differs from, but can be integrated into, walking for transportation. Practitioners as diverse as Buddhist Thich Nhat Hanh and Christian Bruce Epperly have written about the benefits of walking as meditation practice. A walk strengthens the connection with my body and with the world around me. It clears my mind, centers my emotions, and stimulates my imagination. It slows me to a humane pace and restores perspective. All in a matter of steps.

Slowing Down

Contemporary Westerners spend most days at hyper-speed. We glorify multitasking and expect immediate responses to inquiries. We travel in planes, trains, and automobiles—fast. Even the seventy-mile-per-hour speed limits on the interstate feel too slow, so we speed. The digital world changes fast; it obscures the sluggish analog reality. Being trapped in such a culture, we forget that our species evolved in a much slower world. Recovering that slow pace opens us to our own beings.

Walking returns me to the slower-paced world. Often in daily life, I find my mind flitting here and there. I can feel at the mercy of my tumbling thoughts; going along for the ride; jumping between past and future, regret and fret; anticipating what could go wrong; bemoaning what has gone wrong. When I slow down and walk, I try to be exactly where I am. I discover that I can distract my annoying mind and bring it fully into the present, the moment that I actually live in the right now. I let the sights and sounds and smells and sensations engulf and capture me. I admire the texture of the bark of a tree, note the different shades of brick on a house, encounter wisps of the sweet smell of honeysuckle, feel the slants of the pavement beneath my feet, wonder at the diversity of angles of roofs in the same block, hear the giggles and shrieks of children as I approach the playground, feel the cool breeze or the hot sun on my skin. With this type of beginner's mind, searching for what is new or different, even the most familiar routes become an adventure.

Walking a regular daily circuit keeps me engaged with the passing of the seasons and the human changes in my neighborhood. I see the buds slowly growing, until one amazing morning a flower pops out. If I'm early enough, I might spot a moonflower. I notice the shop that's changed its color scheme and see progress in rebuilding the burned-out townhouse up the street. I feel and hear the crunch of dead brown leaves beneath my feet, one of my favorite moments of the year. It's an occasion not to miss.

I learn my neighborhood, the place where I live, as I walk. I learn its weather and climate patterns. I observe the people who live around me, my neighbors. I discover the native flora and fauna, even in the city. In Oklahoma City, I saw possums slinking in early evening. In Manhattan, Kansas, I watched the rabbits that played in the tree-filled yards downtown.

Slowing to a humane speed as I move allows my brain to slow. Instead of cascading forward with worry after worry: Did I remember to send that email? How am I going to get that assignment done by deadline? Did I handle that conversation with my colleague reasonably? What am I going to say to my partner? Thoughts come, as they will, and I notice them, label them as thoughts, and release them, letting them skim the surface layer of my brain like leaves floating on a stream or clouds traversing the sky. I let them be but don't engage with them. Instead, I notice where I am and what is right here before and around me.

Connecting with the Body

Besides connecting with the environment, I connect with my own body. It's moving. What do I notice about my posture, my rate of walking, how my hands and arms move? What do my observations about my body tell me about what I'm feeling? When I'm sad, my walk is slower. When I'm happy—or even more, angry—I move along at a brisker clip. Am I so preoccupied that there is only motion, no noticing? It may take me ten or fifteen minutes to begin to slow down. Why? I ask myself. What does my body have to tell me about myself?

As I age, I notice the twinges of arthritis. I've learned to modify my movement, maybe stopping to stretch, or massage a wrist that feels tender. What do I need to do to take care of this, the only body I have?

I've learned a lot about posture from other movement disciplines like yoga and tai chi. I apply those principles as I walk. Are my shoulders hunched? I open my chest and pull my shoulder blades back. Are my knees turning in? I consciously take each step, keeping my knee directly over my ankle. Are my hips sore? I tilt my pelvis to create a more centered, smoother movement.

Changing the way I am walking can adjust my emotions and open me up to deeper levels of awareness. When I notice my shoulders are hunched and relax them, lifting and opening my chest, suddenly I can see the sky instead of the sidewalk before me. As my body changes, my feelings change. I release the tension, anger, and fear and open myself to joy. I notice the clouds drifting across the blue sky and feel glad to be alive. As my posture changes, I breathe more deeply and find a centered calm as I move.

I practice balance as I walk, noticing as the weight shifts from one foot to the other. Where in my foot does the weight fall—heels, toes, in between? How does my body respond when I hit uneven ground? When I'm going uphill or down? How do I adjust my speed? My stance?

I learn about my body, how it's related to my thoughts and emotions, and how it responds to the world as I walk. I feel the connection of my skin to the movement of the air. I adjust my pace to meet the terrain. I become part of the world I am walking through.

My wish for you is that you find the discipline that brings you the awareness, connection, and wisdom that walking has given me.

questions for your consideration

◆ The author talks about the importance of "noticing" the environment and her own body. How often do you slow down enough to really *notice*? What activities in your life help you to slow down and notice?

◆ How does your body show you how you're feeling? How can you be more aware of it?

◆ There are all kinds of pilgrimages—from the Camino, to a labyrinth walk, to a trip to a place you've always wanted to visit. What would it mean for you to think of your next trip as a pilgrimage? What about simply walking in your neighborhood?

making art

amy zucker morgenstern

When I was a child, I wanted to be an artist. My parents encouraged me with art materials and classes, visits to museums, and my very own drawing table. I even went to a high school for the arts, and one of my majors in college was studio art. After college, I entered a decades-long dry spell, held back by fear and perfectionism, but I knew I was neglecting a source of renewal and wisdom. When I finally heeded the messages telling me that I needed to get back to art, I rediscovered the joy that animated me in childhood. Now I try to dedicate a few hours a week to art. If a spiritual practice is a discipline undertaken to develop wisdom, compassion, love, honesty, courage, faith, and a greater engagement with life, then for me, making art is a spiritual practice.

Art presents all the obstacles of other spiritual practices as well. I can get mired in ego, whether expressed as pride or insecurity. I can stay on the surface, playing around and making something pretty, but shying away from more profound meanings. I can be lazy and go a month without making anything. I can get isolated, avoiding interactions with viewers and other artists for fear of their judgment and my own. All of these hindrances are themselves spiritual lessons.

Inspiration exists, but it has to find you working.
—Pablo Picasso

I had been waiting for an inspiration about an Emily Dickinson poem I loved. I told myself that when the right image came to me, I would make a piece of art. For a couple of months, my designated art time came and went without my doing much of anything. After all, how could I create art without an idea? Then my family and I had a couple of quiet days out of town with friends, with lots of free time. One friend brought a box of art materials: rubber stamps, patterned papers, markers. Despite the blockage I'd been experiencing, they were irresistible. I sat down next to her, still with no idea where to begin, with just the lines of this poem asking for some kind of visual expression. Oh, well, ideas or no ideas, I might as well do something, I thought. I picked up a marker and began to draw a vine, with rubber-stamped letters meandering along it, spelling out the poem's first line. Suddenly I knew that the second line needed to be stamped below it in a contrasting style: each letter in a square, regimented. That brought a new image to mind, that of a circuit board. In the squares between the letters, I drew the filaments of the circuit board marching in formation, then diverging, then turning, mechanical and precise. As I drew, another image popped into my head, and I knew how I was going to illustrate a line from later in the same poem. From a state of no inspiration, I had ideas coming faster than I could record them.

Time and again, I delay making art until I'm really inspired, and time and again, I have to relearn that it usually works the other way around. If I just sit down to it, even if I'm *not* inspired, something thrilling happens: Ideas begin to appear. They emerge seemingly from the work itself; they run up my hand into my brain and begin dancing there and then back through my hand to the paper. For me, a skeptic and a thoroughgoing humanist, it is a profound lesson in grace.

Starting with no ideas, or with one that is half-formed and uncertain, means that art involves lots of dead ends. Lots of time in the studio takes me down paths that lead apparently nowhere or to nothing I like. The process of making several mediocre drawings leads to a few promising ideas, out of which one might eventually blossom into a good drawing. The mediocre work is part of the process, as essential as the good stuff. So the particular piece may be a dead end, but the journey as a whole leads somewhere wonderful.

From learning for myself that Picasso's wisdom holds true in art, I've opened up to the idea that it may be true of spiritual growth in general. We read about epiphanies that come to people out of nowhere, and when I read these accounts, I long for insight to erupt when I am doing something ordinary, like washing the dishes or walking in the woods. I would prefer to skip the preparatory work. And insights *can* break through unexpectedly. But my experience in art suggests that, like seeds, they are most likely to break through prepared ground.

> *The cautious seldom err.*
> —Confucius

> *You must do the thing you think you cannot do.*
> —Eleanor Roosevelt

Most of the time I spend making art I spend making mistakes. The ideas fall flat, the images don't come to life, or I simply don't have the skill to express my vision in charcoal or oil. This is discouraging and tempts me to keep making the same kinds of pieces I know I can do well. If, when I'm being bold, the final creation that ends up on paper usually falls short of the vision in my head, why be bold? So mutters the inner voice of caution. But choosing caution is like sitting down on the spiritual path and refusing to go any farther.

If art is a spiritual path, it leads on. Art challenges me constantly to choose the untrodden way.

Several years ago, during that long dry period in which I had virtually stopped making art, I had a sabbatical from my job as a congregational minister. The time was intended for personal and professional development, with almost complete freedom to decide what would be most educational for me. I decided to face a fear by taking a class in drawing the human figure. When I walked into the studio on the first day, I was almost trembling with the fear of doing it badly and getting it wrong. The results astonished me, not because the drawings were very good—I look at them now and see how stiff and unsure I was—but because *I loved making them.* I enjoyed myself. My fear was not gone—and I still feel an echo of that dread each time I set out to draw what is before me—but having pushed through it, I found the joys of art were there waiting for me.

The regular making of art since then has built up a habit that not only keeps me working at it but has carried bit by bit into the rest of my life. For example, after that sabbatical, I realized that in writing, as in art, too often I had been staying safe, not digging down to know what was deeply heartfelt and express that passion. With the lesson of the figure-drawing studio in mind, I became braver about my sermons: speaking about injustices that keep me awake at night; sharing the vision that gives my life meaning; leaving the shelter of abstractions and generalizations and giving voice instead to the actual fears, hopes, and struggles of the congregation. This continues to feel risky, but I have become emboldened to take more risks as a minister. I am also bolder in my decisions as a parent, partner, friend, and citizen. After developing the risk-taking muscle in art, I could use it elsewhere as well.

Risk and its attendant failures are also a constant instruction in what Buddhism calls nonattachment. When a piece of art is disappointing, I have to let go of the image that I thought would say one thing and seemed to say the opposite; let go of the hours of work poured into a piece because it is dominated by vertical lines and I belatedly realize they need to be diagonal; let go of the brilliant idea in my head that turned out not to be so brilliant once it was on paper; let go of the piece I thought was finished but turned out to be, at most, a lesson in what not to do the next time. Each act of letting go is an acceptance of loss and a surrender of control. This is good for my soul. Loss happens in the rest of life, and when it does, I want to acknowledge and experience it fully. As much as I would like to be in control of the events of my life, it's generally not possible, not with the big things. So the practice of letting go in art making helps me live with more honesty and courage.

Everything vanishes around me, and works are born as if out of the void. Ripe, graphic fruits fall off. My hand has become the obedient instrument of a remote will.
—Paul Klee

I just write 'em as they come.
—Bob Dylan

An image came to my mind recently: many lines, each made up of segments of many colors, tangling and crossing around and behind one central shape of blank white. I had no idea what it might mean (and I do want my art to mean something), but the image was insistent, so I started drawing it. When I finished, I wanted to make another, with blank spaces shaped differently from those in the first piece, so I did that, still not knowing what these pieces might be saying. I didn't feel as much like the creator as like a channel through which creativity flowed. I kept wanting to assert myself as the creator by analyzing what these images might mean and rationally considering what should come next, but I had a feeling I should suspend that process for a while and continue to surrender control. That surrender had brought me thus far, and thanks to it, I encountered images that came from beyond myself.

By the time I finished the second piece, I knew that what spoke to me most in them was the way the blank shapes emerged without being explicitly outlined. The way they were only implied and yet so powerfully present: That meant something. It evoked experiences of the things in life that are not clearly visible and hard to put into words but that have great power and presence: forces such as love, fear, and hope. Now that I had reflected on what those images meant, I could generate new images that emphasized that meaning. But I couldn't bring my analytical mind to express the significance of the art until I had trustingly followed those images for a time.

The process of making art is full of surprises if I let myself be a channel for whatever may come. Where does this stream of creativity originate? I have no idea. In most areas of life, I am a pretty rational person, using my mind, using words, making plans, building my skills, trying to comprehend how things work. When I'm making art, a different element enters. There, my job is to hone my craft and then let my hand be moved by mysterious forces. I step into mystery and float where its current takes me.

> *. . . here there is no place*
> *that does not see you. You must change your life.*
> —Rainer Maria Rilke

Except sometimes, when I refuse to float. This resistance often kicks in shortly after the thrill of having discovered unexpected wisdom through a piece I'm making. Something in the work tells me, "You must change your life." If I am making a piece about the powerful presence of things unseen, then the change may demand that I exercise faith in ways I have never been comfortable doing. If I am working on a series of drawings of erosion and decay, it may prime me to notice the beauty and worth in things I had initially thought ugly—an openness that extends to how I see people, and so now I must treat people differently. This is exactly what I hope art will do: transform me and possibly viewers. Yet at times, even as I am making the art, I resist the transformation. Engulfed by mystery, I already feel as if I'm in over my head, and I want to do anything but wade in deeper—go have a cup of tea, read about art instead of making it, wash the dishes, write in my blog. The discipline of art cajoles me to take a deep breath and continue to make, to listen, to change.

> *The sculptor Giacometti was commissioned by the French Government to design a coin in commemoration of the artist Henri Matisse. He spent five full days in Matisse's bedroom sketching and sketching the old artist. Drawing after drawing displeased Giacometti and finally he shouted in despair, "Oh Master, I cannot draw," and Matisse replied, "None of us can."*
> —told by Paulus Berensohn

I am standing at an easel, charcoal in hand, awed by the beauty of the model before us. His body is ordinary enough, but in the light of attention, the ordinary is anything but commonplace. Every muscle carries the promise of movement; every square inch of skin bears a history of the things he has felt and done. To attempt to translate all of that and more into lines of black and gray seems an awesome task, both necessary and impossible. To make him live on paper, as he does here in this room, for others to contemplate and perhaps understand, is an act of reverence and love. It also seems to be beyond my ability.

At the moments when I seem to be attempting the impossible, I comfort myself with the story about Giacometti and

Matisse. If they believed they could not draw, then maybe I'm being too hard on myself. Maybe what makes so many artists cry out, "I cannot draw!"—including those far, far more talented than I—is the sheer beauty and complexity of the world, too sublime to be imitated. Somehow this is reassuring. It turns my attention away from achievement and puts it on the process of drawing itself: just being there, together with the object or person or landscape or fall of light that is before me, and the beauty that I have been given to perceive. This, I realize, is my aim in drawing in the first place: just to be, to be aware, to give attention to whatever is present. To be present.

In drawing a piece of the world, I strive to pay attention, moment by moment. When I put down my materials and get up from the chair, my vision has changed. The world outside is more vivid; details emerge that I have never noticed before. I can't claim to walk around in a state of perfect awareness. Much too often, I still rush through the world, missing its beauty while my mind is occupied with my to-do list or my eyes are on my cellphone. But gradually, the practice of giving attention through drawing has expanded my perception and opened my heart to beauty and wonder.

Once in a while, as I contemplate the model and trying to draw what I see, a miracle occurs. I draw a curve that is so precisely the one I am looking at that I experience a micro-moment of confusion: Which is the drawing and which is the model? It passes, and I am back to attempting the impossible, but for that instant, something that seemed apart from me has become a part of me, and I a part of it.

> *Creativity takes courage.*
> —Henri Matisse

With so much of my art making time devoted to mistakes, I'm often discouraged by failure, and frequently I want to quit: This drawing doesn't look like the model, this collage doesn't look like what was in my mind, my sculpture has collapsed, I'm no good at this, it's hopeless. Sometimes I do quit. Conceiving of art as a spiritual practice, not just a hobby, nudges me to give a long sigh and summon the courage to start again.

Making art is about going deeper into reality. In representational art, that means drawing what I see; in abstract work, it means a disciplined examination of my own mind and beliefs. To know whether an image honestly reflects what I am trying to say, I need to *know* what I am trying to say. The process interrogates me: What do I believe? Why? Is it even true? At moments when I would rather evade those questions, the practice of making art helps keep me honest.

For example, recently I have been making small drawings that are all variations on grids. I'm interested in bending the lines of the grid, or making some squares so big that they seem to stretch and distort the whole network, or letting the lines of the squares fly apart, all while still keeping the grid recognizably a grid. The tension between the formal rules of the grid and the movement that arises through and in spite of that form evoke all sorts of other tensions in my mind: To what extent are our lives ordered or chaotic, regimented or free, communal or individual? Do I believe these qualities exist in tension and balance with each other, in the way the drawings imply? When does a grid cease to be a grid, its lines pulled into fragments? When does a community cease to be a community because its elements have flown too far apart? I want my drawings to speak my truth, and for that to happen I need to question what I am saying and what I believe. The drawings are simple to make, but the ideas are hard to contemplate.

I link my work to the social struggle. But as my principal weapon in this struggle is my work, I take it very seriously and do everything to ennoble it.
—Leopoldo Méndez

For me, a spiritual practice must have an ethical dimension. If it doesn't help me act with more justice and kindness, then its benefits are locked within the borders of myself and it is mere self-improvement rather than spiritual growth. Great art is often directly related to the social struggle for more justice, freedom, and equality. I both love this kind of art and participate in this struggle as a minister and activist. My own art has seldom been overtly political in content, but just the same, I want it to do its part to change the world by working upon me as the maker and upon others as viewers.

The practice of making art, at its best, leads me simultaneously inward and outward. Drawing a hummingbird resting on a wire has made me feel akin to the bird and determined to protect its habitat. In my grief about the fire in my region that killed dozens of people who had been forced by scarcity into unsafe housing, I begin obsessively drawing narrowing, burning shapes. Spending time with the images compels me to become more active in addressing the housing crisis in my region. The drawings about unseen forces that I mentioned earlier: Making them has helped me look below the surface of social interactions and see the structures of power and privilege that shape these interactions. Perhaps the art can have these effects on others when they see it. But even if no one else ever saw it, its effect on me would have its impact on the world by sending me forth with a bit more compassion and wisdom.

This spiritual practice alters my character. As I have described, making art requires me to set aside doubt and move through fear; this habit prepares me to be bolder in acting for justice. When I draw a person or animal, it is a sustained exercise in empathy; that muscle, strengthened, helps me to respond with compassion to others' experiences and to be persuaded of my responsibilities toward other beings. When I make abstract art, I am frequently envisioning a different world and trying to make it live on paper or in clay; this is a spiritual skill that improves my activism. And my practice brings me again and again to awareness of how precious and fragile life is, strengthening my commitment to preserve what is good.

Me: *I'm trying to write about why I make art.*
Indigo Morgenstern (my daughter): *Because it's fun!*

My daughter is right. I'm at my happiest when I'm playing with color, cutting out shapes for a collage, trying this and that, shaping clay (my undergraduate work was in ceramics, and I used to say I majored in playing with mud). Art makes me feel free to go wherever I want, invent worlds and play in them. It's fun! Yet a Puritan streak in me protests at this idea. Aren't spiritual practices supposed to be difficult? In an essay called "Banging on the Doors of Heaven: A Brief Meditation on Spiritual Practices," retired Unitarian Universalist minister James Ishmael Ford writes that for an activity to be a spiritual practice, it needs to entail intention, attention, repetition, and correction. I agree—and if a spiritual practice meets these requirements, it is bound to be challenging. Yet, with such a wide world of possible spiritual practices to choose from, there is no reason not to choose one that immerses us in enjoyment, joy, beauty, playfulness, pleasure, and satisfaction even as it provides that challenge.

Making art isn't *always* enjoyable. It brings me face-to-face with reality, which is often grim and frightening. It compels me to do things I don't do well and confront my own ignorance. It pries my controlling fingers off the steering wheel, coaxing me to surrender to the mystery that moves through everything. It frequently entails just plain discouragement and difficulty. It's a good thing making art *is* so much fun, or I would never plow on through the hard parts. The moments of pure enjoyment sustain my practice. It has been my good fortune to have found, and been encouraged in, a spiritual practice that is sustainable, and that sustains me in the lifelong daily effort to become a better person who will help make a better world.

questions for your consideration

◆ What is your relationship with art? Is it a part of your life, or has the voice(s) that says, "I'm not an artist" won the day?

◆ If you had to choose, what kind of art would you create? Drawings? Paintings? Sculpture? Photographs? Mosaics? Why? What would it take to try?

◆ The author writes that making art has taught her about courage, surrender, noticing and appreciating, and honesty. What else could you imagine it teaching *you*?

◆ How might you integrate a practice like this into your own life?

◆ The author writes about having reintroduced art into her life after a long hiatus. Is there a practice from your past that you might rekindle?

creating community

jessica lin

I recently attended an energizing Unitarian Universalist Young Adult Group lunch that had me grinning from ear to ear. We had several visitors at the gathering, who marveled at how they felt welcomed into the congregation on their very first visit. People greeted them warmly and told them about various groups they might be interested in joining. They had come to our fellowship specifically because they were seeking community, and they were so heartened to discover our Young Adult Group. I loved hearing that. Being intentional about creating community is close to my heart and has become a guiding philosophy and spiritual practice for me, which is surprising given my past.

I used to be vehemently against joining things and being a part of community. In high school, I was so proud of being a loner, of being what I thought was fiercely independent. Growing up, I had always been quiet, introverted, bookish, and more than a little socially awkward, but I always had a few close friends whom I could count on. Then, in high school, I distanced myself from my little group of friends and started spending my lunch period either in the library or outside, sitting underneath a giant tree. I still had my best friend to talk to, but I sequestered myself from a lot of other people.

In college, thankfully, I ended my self-imposed isolation but still felt wary about joining social groups, especially religious or Asian-American ones. I didn't want to be one of those Asian Americans who only hung out with other Asian Americans. I looked down on them, maybe out of an unfortunate desire to feel assimilated into white American society. I avoided religious groups out of disenchantment with the evangelical church community I had grown up in, especially because of their intolerance for LGBTQ folks.

After college, I moved to another city, where I was a stranger. I felt so intensely lonely. I went to work, stayed late, and then came home to work some more. Being a lifelong bookworm, I tackled my problem of loneliness by going to the library and checking out books on how people found friends. I read works like *Loneliness: Human Nature and the Need for Social Connection* by John T. Cacioppo and William Patrick; *Lonely: A Memoir* by Emily White, which made me cry; and *MWF Seeking BFF: My Yearlong Search for a New Best Friend* by Rachel Bertsche. I tortured myself by reading beautifully written books about wonderful female friendships, including Ann Patchett's memoir *Truth & Beauty: A Friendship*. I followed online comments on sites like Metafilter that gave advice on how to build friendships from acquaintanceships.

I took in the advice from the books and online commentators, and I thought about what my interests were and where I could find people who shared them. After some digging, I found a local book club. We met once a month, and I got to know some of the other members a little better. Eventually, we became close enough to start hanging out together outside of book club, getting coffee or having dinner. I also started going to the local Unitarian Universalist congregation, the first UU church I had ever attended. The warmth and humor there caught me off guard. I loved that there was plenty of laughter and chuckling during services, how people were encouraged to share their personal joys and sorrows out loud during the service, and how they were then held and supported by the congregation. I attended only on Sundays.

While I longed to join the choir and participate in other activities that I read about in the bulletin, my work schedule did not permit me to get more involved.

I moved back to my hometown a few years later and again faced the challenge of creating community, but this time it didn't seem as daunting since I was in familiar surroundings and had family nearby. I threw myself into it with gusto, joining the local UU congregation and attending the Wednesday night programs there. I also participated in a few Meetup book clubs and made some amazing friends through them. Discussing books about life and mortality and relationships brought out the tender side of the members. They were willing to share their hopes, fears, and regrets.

After one of the discussions, a woman who had recently moved to the area struck up a conversation with me as we walked out of the coffee shop. She said that she was interested in meeting and getting to know people better. So we exchanged phone numbers and email addresses. I was impressed by her forthrightness and sense of mission about creating community. It can be quite difficult to make friends at any age, but especially in the post-college years, when old friends have scattered to all parts of the country following jobs and partners. I've had many conversations with other young adults who are struggling with this. Just talking about it has helped us feel less alone and less like outcasts.

As I began to know people in my book clubs better and felt less lonely, I was able to turn a more discerning eye to the types of books we were reading. I realized that they were primarily books written by white men and women. Craving more diversity, I started my own book club that would read books written only by authors of color. I created a Meetup group and started scouring the Internet for book lists and suggestions. We began with *The Sympathizer* by Viet Thanh Nguyen and went on to *Kindred* by Octavia Butler. We read nonfiction like *The Warmth of Other Suns: The Epic Story of America's Great*

Migration by Isabel Wilkerson, and invited members to share how their own lives were reflected by those on the page, how their families had made journeys out of the South. It was a revelation to read about a part of our country's history that isn't in the textbooks and to hear the oral history of people's lives from just a generation or two ago. I was moved, educated, and enlightened. We slowly became familiar with each other's struggles and triumphs. My book club introduced me to people of different ages, backgrounds, experiences, races, and ethnicities; hearing their stories has enriched my life.

I heard about an Asian-American activist group in the area and attended a few of their events. One of these included a timeline exercise in which we responded to past civil rights events with our own written reflections. One of the reflections stood out to me so much that I keep it in my planner: "Distancing ourselves from other people of color only results in our continued marginalization." I am only now slowly learning how powerful and rejuvenating it is to spend time with other people of color.

The music director at my congregation, Yuri Yamamoto, told me about a Unitarian Universalist racial justice retreat for young adults. I attended Grow Racial Justice as part of the Thrive Young Adults of Color cohort. This expanded my idea of what a UU community could be. We allowed ourselves to be vulnerable and shared our spiritual journeys with one another, examining what it meant to be young adults of color and Unitarian Universalists. I felt challenged, embraced, and energized to work for justice. A truly life-changing experience. It was so moving and meaningful that I decided to attend again a second summer to meet new people and deepen my faith even further.

Inspired by a conversation with a friend from another UU congregation whom I met at Grow Racial Justice, I have started a People of Color Affinity group at my own congregation. It's small but has given me strength and support.

Having transformed from someone who shied away from connection and community to a person who became a joiner and then a creator of community, I have now decided that I want to deepen my existing relationships. It does seem strange as an adult to have to think so intentionally about friendships. In childhood, my friends were often those who sat next to me, lived near me, or whose parents were friends with my parents. But with so many demands on us—jobs, partners, families, volunteer commitments—it takes work to carve out time and to be the one who initiates get-togethers. Sometimes if I've had a really busy week or two, I have to resurface, breathe, and realize that the reason I feel so out of sorts is that I haven't seen some close friends in a while. So I'll email or text someone about grabbing brunch or I'll have some people over for a game night, reminding myself that the food doesn't have to be perfect and the house doesn't have to be immaculate. What matters is the company, the laughter, the sharing. To relieve the stress of having to prepare a lot of food, I'll have potlucks on the game nights.

If any of this appeals to you and you've had the same kinds of struggles I've had, here are some ways to create community:

- Join an existing group or community. This can be a religious community, volunteer group, or a common interest group. Meetup.com is a great resource for interest groups: for hiking, dining out, seeing comedy shows, writing, attending plays or movies, learning how to dance, or doing woodworking. Anything and everything under the sun. Find a hobby that interests you, or try something new.
- If you have an idea for something that doesn't exist yet, create it! As in the movie *Field of Dreams*, if you build it, they will come.

- Foster one-on-one connections, and build deeper relationships. Go for a walk in the park, or have coffee or a meal with a friend. Turn off your phone, and give your friend and the conversation your full attention.
- Find an online community that you could enjoy participating in.
- Create a long-standing weekly or monthly get-together, whether it is a board game night, trivia night, karaoke, or dinner party.
- Connect friends from different groups, but don't force friendships if the people aren't interested.
- Remember to build in time for being alone. I like to walk in the park and sing show tunes in the car.
- When you meet someone you find to be a kindred spirit, be sure to get their contact information and then invite them to the next event you're hosting. You could even have personal business cards to hand out.
- Invite people you'd like to know better to events you would have attended anyway, like museum exhibits, movie showings, or author book readings.
- Have a cookie party, especially during the holidays. Invite people over and ask them to each bring a dozen cookies. Everyone can try the different types and bring the combined assortments home.
- Call friends who live farther away or write a letter to a friend you haven't communicated with for a while.
- Send a friend an article via email you think they might enjoy.
- Lend a favorite book of yours.

Being part of a community is about being seen, being heard, being held, and holding others. Creating community has brought so much joy to my life and has become a spiritual practice. I know that friends will come and go. But when we share our stories, our histories, and give and receive support, we experience true blessings.

questions for consideration

◆ Do you find it difficult to create and nurture new friendships as the author describes? If so, what do you see as some of the challenges?

◆ The author says that being part of a community is about, "being seen, being heard, being held, and holding others." Is there anything you would add to or change about that description?

◆ Where in your life do you currently find your deepest experience of belonging? Why do you think you do?

◆ How could you see yourself integrating the practice of creating community into your life?

collecting joy as a spiritual practice

ann richards

I have struggled to recognize joy my whole adult life. While I try not to be a "Debbie Downer," I have always veered toward the pessimistic and skeptical. This all began to change one gloomy spring day, when I was sitting in front of a keyboard for the umpteenth hour in a beige-colored office accented with fluorescent lighting. I was working for the estimable Rev. Ginger Luke, who encouraged me to leave my computer and come out with her to the front lawn. I was feeling overwhelmed with work and didn't want to stop typing, but grumbling to myself, I followed her. There, alongside the walkway leading to the church was a small, lonely purple flower. I thought it sort of sad and underwhelming and was considering something polite to say when I looked up at Ginger. It wasn't the purple flower that was noteworthy. It was Ginger's face. She brightened looking at it, her mouth became a dimple-punctuated smile, and her enthusiastic words encouraged me to "Look! Look!" Watching Ginger's joy was contagious, and I began to feel joyful myself. Walking back indoors, I didn't have a dowdy office; I had a shared space with my excellent friend Beth. I had good music on and was making progress with my projects. I felt joyful.

Not long afterward, I turned on my car radio to hear John Mayall singing "Room to Move." I cranked up the volume, smiled, and car-danced all the way home. I felt truly joyful, listening to that amazing harmonica solo, and remembering how my father would lean closer to the speakers to better focus on this song as he listened to it. Again, I found myself experiencing joy through others, a great discovery for someone who had been immune to feelings anywhere approaching something like joy. I began to conscientiously collect moments of joy that I could relive and treasure as a way to awaken joy in myself. Collecting moments of joy has become a spiritual practice for me.

It began with memories. Instead of lying in bed at night stewing about the thing I shouldn't have said, I purposefully reviewed memories of absolute joy I had experienced, including Ginger and the purple flower and my father listening to John Mayall. Then, while watching Gene Kelly's performance of "Singin' in the Rain" in the movie, I realized that I could collect more than memories. I could collect artifacts: movies, videos, books, music, all of people expressing their joy. I now have a file on my computer marked "Joy" for email artifacts to review on days when I'm feeling blue and a collection of video artifacts on YouTube at home for the same purpose.

The collection requires very little thought. I can call up the memories anywhere and anytime and easily collect lists and files of the artifacts to refer to. What I found to be more complicated was identifying what would go into my collection. To assist in this, I have certain guidelines for myself to choose appropriate examples of joy for my collection: Something is a spiritual practice only if you make it one, and I try to make my practice both special and particular.

First, I don't include mere happiness in my collection. I know that some equate peace or serenity with joy. That's not what I'm talking about. Happiness has its place and deserves its own list. Of course, this is completely subjective, but I'm looking for things that inspire unbridled, unbounded joy. I'm looking for things that so engross me with positive feeling, I can only focus on them for that moment and everything else is shut out. I'm looking for things that leave me with a warm feeling and a smile, even when the experience is over. I'm looking for enthusiasm, unmitigated élan. I am talking about the wide-eyed, panting, bop, bang, boom of Animal the Muppet playing the drums. If you are too young to remember this reference, or need a refresher, check him out on YouTube. There is an interview with Animal viewable online, and he says that the two things he loves the most in this world are drums and bunny rabbits. He's a fictional character, but I believe him! His drum playing gives the viewer a vicarious thrill. I have no interest in playing drums, but watching Animal do what he loves gives me a new sense of what joy can be.

My second "joy moment" guideline is that I am not restricted to feelings that originate with me. I believe that joy is infectious. I am more successful in identifying moments for my collection if I start by looking for it in others. There is nothing wrong with recognizing joy elsewhere and taking it on for yourself. A wonderful example is a flash mob. If you haven't had the experience of a really good flash mob, you can again check YouTube.

I've become sort of a flash mob connoisseur. My favorites online include all kinds of people and lots of amazed onlookers. They build and build until you find yourself grinning and wishing you could have been there yourself. In a way, a flash mob that grows from one person to two, to six, to twenty, to one hundred is a manifestation of this very point: That joy doesn't need to originate with you. You can get it from others.

Another of my personal guidelines for finding joy expressed by others is that I don't have to share in the source of that joy. Whatever made that other person joyful doesn't need to be something that I find inspirational myself. For example, the Edwin Hawkins Singers exude joy in their great gospel song, "Oh Happy Day." I'm not a born-again Christian, and I don't share the religious fervor that inspired Edwin Hawkins to write this song. But it doesn't matter. I can hear the joy in it, and that's enough. Similarly, I didn't see the art exhibit that inspired Modest Mussorgsky to create the piano compositions *Paintings at an Exhibition*, but I recognize joy when I hear his piece, "The Gates of Kiev."

When I'm collecting moments of joy for future reference and rumination I do not include weddings and births and other such life events. This doesn't mean I don't find joy in them. I do, but there is a certain *assumption* that those events will offer joy to participants. In my search for joy, I get to decide what is joyful, with no expectations.

Sometimes, during the holiday season, for example, many feel a tyranny of prescribed joy. We are expected to find joy at specific events and in particular ways, and those who experienced a loss before the holiday season or dread turning a certain age, for example, may not find the associated celebrations to be joyful at all. I find it more fulfilling to collect my own moments of joy, seasonally related or not. I prefer to collect them as a spiritual practice and examine them to nourish my own spirit without reference to cultural norms.

An excellent explanation of this point of view is in Byrd Baylor's beautiful picture book, *I'm in Charge of Celebrations*. She explains how she creates her own holidays based on the moments in her life she most wants to remember. I added this artifact to my joy collection the very first time I read it.

In my life, I have worked hard on political campaigns, and sometimes my candidates have won. That kind of joy is worth remembering and savoring, but I don't include those moments in my spiritual practice collection. While I was full of joy, of necessity someone else was miserable. If it is joy at another's expense, it falls into a different category.

So, to summarize my parameters for collecting joyful moments:

◆ It's more than happiness.

◆ It should be infectious.

◆ The source of the joy doesn't need to be inspirational to me.

◆ Weddings, births, and similar life events aren't included.

◆ Joy at another's expense doesn't qualify.

Our capacity to capture spontaneous moments of joy has recently exploded exponentially, thanks to the Internet. For example, in 1938, bass player Bob Haggart and drummer Ray Bauduc were performing with the Bobcats. After their first set at the Blackhawk Nightclub, Bob and Ray came back early from their break to tune instruments and set up for the next set. Bob was whistling and slapping the bass, and Ray was backing him up on drums. People came back from the bar when they heard and started cheering them on. The audience grew as the whistle developed into an improvised melody. They started clapping and shouting encouragement, and Ray went into a drum solo. There was such excitement about what was happening that Ray continued to play and, looking around for something else to drum on, began to play the bass strings with his drumsticks while Bob played the melody with his left hand. The crowd went wild, and the whole event became legendary. The tune they improvised that night, "Big Noise from Winnetka," became a byword for a joyful jazz experience, a perfect synchronicity among listeners, drummer, and bassist. Bob and Ray performing "Big Noise from Winnetka" were subsequently captured on film, as audiences everywhere wanted to know what the fuss was about. While the films are undeniably fun to watch, obviously they do not capture the wild excitement of the first, improvised experience.

We can never know what that joy was truly like; it spontaneously grew out of the moment. That has been the case for the past forty thousand years, until just the past decade.

We'll never know what the famous opera singer Jenny Lind sounded like, or how the great Edmond Keene interpreted Hamlet. But the technology of the past decade allows us to capture moments of joy as they happen and share them.

We can create a spiritual practice of collecting moments of joy, and with technology we can have a second communal practice of sharing these artifacts. One reason we come to church on Sunday mornings is to hear live music and experience joy together, among many other sensations. But we are privileged in that we can hear not only live music on Sunday mornings but also Anna Maffo's version of *Songs of the Auvergne*, or Katrina and the Waves' "Walking on Sunshine." We can discover moments of joy that took place when we were not there originally, and in addition we can share artifacts of joyful experiences with others who were not there.

The spiritual practice of collecting moments of joy has grown for me as I share them with the people I love. They may not feel the same sense of joy I do when listening, looking, and sharing, but they do get to know a little more about me, and I have the wonderful feeling of enjoying those moments again with those I care about.

Share links of your favorite music to friends you haven't seen in a while, share photos of your joyful moments in nature with homebound congregants, or read a poem over Skype to a friend. To keep the moments that bring you true joy to yourself is a lost opportunity. And, if you haven't ever heard John Mayall's harmonica solo in "Room to Move," I will perform my spiritual kindness of the day and recommend it to you.

questions for your consideration

◆ Do you tend to really take note of the moments of joy in your life, or are they overshadowed by more difficult things and times?

◆ What, for you, is the difference between "joy" and "happiness"?

◆ What do you think of the author's "joy collection guidelines"? Would you change her list in any way?

◆ How might you integrate a practice like this into your own life?

◆ How do you define joy in your life? How do you know it when you experience it?

integrating technology into spiritual practice

aaron m. stockwell

At five o'clock in the afternoon on a fall afternoon in 2011, I am sitting in a meeting room at the First Unitarian Church in Chicago, Illinois. I am at the first of several important interviews in a minister's career. My cellphone begins to ring. My heart sinks. I'm a seminarian, I think to myself. I know to be respectful. Why did I forget to turn off my alarm?

Minutes before, I had described my spiritual practice to my interviewers as the time that I called "holy questions," where I had set questions as the alarm titles on my cellphone. "Remember that spiritual practice alarm I told you about?" "Yes," the committee responds. "Well, that's one of them." The committee members laugh. A quick-witted member asks, "What does it say?" "Breathe!" "Good advice!" they say. So I do. More centered than before, I complete the interview. After what felt like an eternity (but really fifteen minutes), the committee informs me that I am a candidate for the Unitarian Universalist ministry.

At eight o'clock, I'm at a Thai restaurant with colleagues who have also been granted status as candidates. My phone vibrates. The alarm that comes up on the screen has a question: How have you felt the divine today? A simple question.

I can think of many times when I felt the divine that day. It helps me recall the committee meeting, colleagues, and the works of art I looked at earlier that morning.

These alarms always catch me by surprise, even though they happen throughout the day, every day. There it is again, I chuckle, arriving when you least expect it.

Some may say that spiritual practices and technology don't mix. If spiritual practice is only defined as like the practices of the Christian Desert Mothers and Fathers of the fourth century or those of Buddhist monks, and if we only define technology as something like Instagram, Twitter, or an Apple Watch, then perhaps the two don't mix. But objects like mala beads for counting mantras as they are recited, or rosary beads for Roman Catholics, or Bibles from a printing press for *lectio divina* were all new technology at one time.

Technology is the medium.

Holy Questions at Holy Times

When I started seeing a spiritual director during seminary, I realized that it would be good to remember the questions he was asking me throughout the day. Wondering how I might do this, I realized that I could set up alarms on my smartphone. Much in the way that someone might label when to take medicine or to take the recycling out on Monday night at 8 p.m., I could set certain reminders for myself. When the alarm sounded, the name popped up. For many years, I set four alarms on my smartphone to go off at different times throughout the day. I was able to label each with a question. My practice at the time only included reflecting on the questions silently for a moment and then continuing about my daily tasks, but surely you could turn it into a journaling practice, perhaps tweeting the response to the question or writing the answer down.

The times that I set my alarm to go off varied, but usually were 8:30 a.m., 12:30 p.m., 5:00 p.m., and 9:30 p.m. The questions or prompts varied as well.

The practice can be easily replicated. Try out some different statements or questions; then wait a week or two until you change them. Set your alarms for times where they aren't likely to be a distraction. Some possible topics are:

- What will you do for others this day?
- You are loved.
- Be sure to sing today.
- What have you done for yourself this day?
- What has made you laugh?
- Pay attention.
- How did you feel the divine?
- What or who are you grateful for?
- What brought you joy?
- Slow down.
- Breathe.
- Quiet your mind.
- Be still.

Mindfulness through "Hashtagging"

The *Oxford English Dictionary* defines a hashtag as "[on social media web sites and applications] a word or phrase preceded by a hash and used to identify messages relating to a specific topic; [also] the hash symbol itself, when used in this way." If I were to open Instagram and search for #bluesky, I would get all of the public pictures that users have hashtagged with Blue Sky. If I were to search for #joy, I would find all of the public pictures that users have taken of scenes that have brought them joy. At the time of this writing, the most common social networking sites to use hashtags are Twitter, Facebook, and Instagram.

People often share Advent or Lenten practices online, in which they invite users to take a picture of a scene, object, or person that reminds them of the practice during each day of the Christian liturgical seasons. Seeing what other users think about regarding a particular hashtag can be fascinating.

Many Unitarian Universalist congregations have begun using worship themes that last for a month. Try posting throughout the month various pictures of scenes or objects related to the theme and using a hashtag. At the end of the month, look back to see everything that you posted related to the theme.

Altars in Our Pockets

The practice of building and making altars or shrines is very old. Many people find it meaningful to have a collection of sacred objects in a special spot. Computer desktop images and smart lock screens or wallpaper can be another way to have a visible and visual reminder of what is most important to us at all times. My current lock screen image is a particularly beautiful sunset in the mountains of West Texas.

Mindful Usage

A social media or technology sabbath is about bringing intentionality and mindfulness to how we use technology. Certain apps on our smartphones are called "infinity apps." These apps get us stuck into an infinite loop, such as web browsers, Twitter, Facebook, email, Instagram, and so on. They have a constant stream of information. You can always delete them or disable them if they provide too much information.

Studies have shown that the blue light from smartphone or computer screens can disrupt our sleep patterns. The light that comes from a computer screen is designed to look like the sun. If you are looking at a screen at 10 p.m. or 3 a.m., it is probably not matching the sunlight. There are apps for nearly every device that change the color of the light to match your indoor lighting.

Keeping the Sabbath

The beautiful thing about technology is that it allows us to be in contact with everyone immediately. The frustrating thing about technology is that it allows us to be in contact with everyone immediately.

As I write these words, a few days after the 2016 presidential election, I am in a constant state of information overload and despair. Online, I am getting into arguments with people I don't know well; I am reading articles that are causing me to despair for this world. The information overload is not only due to the election. It also includes phone calls, various church emails, and text messages from friends; the list goes on.

Just as we can spiritually benefit from technology, we also need to unplug from it on a regular basis, take a technology Sabbath. This practice is much like the ancient practice of fasting and self-denial.

Some surveys show that people who abstain from using the Internet or electronic devices experience similar results as those who give up alcohol or smoking. You might be thrilled to receive news, emails, or notifications at any time of the day, but you might find it exhausting as well. So, perhaps once a week, log off all your social networks, delete the app icons from your smartphone, turn off the notifications for email, and observe a technology Sabbath.

These are just a few ways that the use of technology can be integrated into your daily or weekly spiritual practices. Likely there are ways of doing it that I haven't even thought of. As the years go on, new technologies will be invented, and commonplace technologies will have fallen by the wayside.

Many of the spiritual practices in this book could have technology integrated into them. And as technology continues to advance, it will bring new opportunities for us to use it for nurturing our spiritual selves.

questions for your consideration

- Have you ever thought of your phone or tablet as an altar or a call to prayer, meditation, or reflection?

- Does the idea of a "technology Sabbath" resonate with you in any way?

- How might you use your technological devices to support your spiritual practice or *as* your spiritual practice?

resources

Here are some suggested books to read and websites to visit to learn more about the practices described in this book.

Learning to Pray

Help, Thanks, Wow: The Three Essential Prayers by Anne Lamott, Penguin, 2012.

How Do You Pray? Inspiring Responses from Religious Leaders, Spiritual Guides, Healers, Activists & Other Lovers of Humanity edited by Celeste Yacoboni, Monkfish Book Publishing, 2014.

Simply Pray: A Modern Spiritual Practice to Deepen Your Life by Erik Walker Wikstrom, Skinner House Books, 2012.

Finding a Teacher

If You're Lucky Your Heart Will Break: Field Notes from a Zen Life by James Ishmael Ford, Wisdom Publications, 2012.

Shalem Institute for Spiritual Formation: **shalem.org**

Zen Mountain Monastery: **zmm.mro.org**

Directed Mini-Retreats

Retreat Finder: **retreatfinder.com**

The Unitarian Universalist Spiritual Director's Network: **uusdn.org**

Spiritual Directors International: **sdiworld.org**

The Greatest of These Is Love

Unitarian Universalist Mystics in Community: **uumystics.org** and on Facebook.

UU Mystical Experiences, edited by Susan Manker (pamphlet): **http://bit.ly/203WhU6**

Entering the Labyrinth

The Healing Labyrinth: Finding Your Path to Inner Peace by Helen Raphael Sands, Barron's, 2001.

The Labyrinth Society: **labyrinthsociety.org**

Labyrinths for the Spirit: How to Create Your Own Labyrinths for Meditation and Enlightenment by Jim Buchanan, Gaia Books, 2007.

Judith Tripp and the Women's Dream Quest: **circleway.com**

Veriditas—Home of the Labyrinth Movement: **veriditas.org**

Walking a Sacred Path: Rediscovering the Labyrinth as a Spiritual Practice, Revised edition, by Lauren Artress, Penguin, 2006.

Worldwide labyrinth locator: **labyrinthlocator.com**

My Cosmala

Cosmala page: **solstice-and-equinox.com/universebeads.html**

The Great Story Beads page:
thegreatstory.org/great_story_beads.html

The History of the Universe in 10 Minutes: **YouTube**

Our Story in 1 Minute: **YouTube**

Making Magical Moments

For more on the science of bubbles, see "The Chemistry (and a Little Physics) of Soap Bubbles," by David A Katz: **http://bit.ly/2BthejH**

Playing with My Dolls

Erik Walker Wikstrom's photographs of his action figures are posted on his Flickr page: **http://bit.ly/2F4Pyp6**

Roller Derby

Dawn Cooley's blog: **dawncooley.com**

Chop, Chop, Chopping

The Book of New Family Traditions: How to Create Great Rituals for Holidays and Every Day by Meg Cox, Running Press, 2003.

Full Circle: Fifteen Ways to Grow Life-long UUs by Kate Erslev, Skinner House Books, 2004.

Crafting Calm: Projects and Practices for Creativity and Contemplation by Maggie Shannon, Viva Publications, 2013.

The Bloom of the Present Moment

Walden by Henry David Thoreau, Macmillan Collector's Library, 2016.

Wherever You Go, There You Are: Mindfulness Meditation in Everyday Life by Jon Kabat-Zinn, Hyperion Books, 1994.

Meditations by Marcus Aurelius, Dover, 1997.

Walking

"It Will Be Solved in the Walking: Reflections on Martin Sheen's 'The Way' and the Lenten Spiritual Journey" by Bruce G. Epperly: **bobcornwall.com/2012/02/it-will-be-solved-in-walking-bruce.html**

The Long Road Turns to Joy: A Guide to Walking Meditation by Thich Nhat Hanh, Parallax Press, 2011.

The Pilgrimage by Paulo Coelho, HarperCollins, 2009.

A Pilgrim's Guide to the Camino de Santiago: St. Jean, Roncesvalle, Santiago by John Brierley, Findhorn Press, 2010.

"Thich Nhat Hanh on Walking Meditation": **lionsroar.com/how-to-meditate-thich-nhat-hanh-on-walking-meditation**

"The Way," film, starring Martin Sheen, directed by Emilio Estevez

Collecting Joy

"Big Noise from Winnetka" performed by Bob Haggart and Ray Bauduc: **YouTube**

"Do Re Mi" dance performance in Central Station Antwerp: **YouTube**

I'm in Charge of Celebrations by Byrd Baylor, Atheneum Books, 2013.

"The Muppets Theme Song" performed by OK Go, featuring Animal: **YouTube**

"Oh Happy Day" performed by The Edwin Hawkins Singers: **YouTube**

"Pictures at an Exhibition" by Modest Mussorgsky: **YouTube**

"Room to Move" performed by John Mayall: **YouTube**

Integrating Technology

Resources for social media Sabbaths are available from the Church of the Larger Fellowship: **http://bit.ly/clf-sabbath**

about the contributors

Lynn M. Acquafondata is a licensed mental health counselor in private practice in Rochester, New York. In addition to her work with individuals, couples, and families, she has created the Congogram Congregational Counseling process. An ordained minister, she has served congregations and worked as a hospice chaplain.

Matt Alspaugh came into ministry as a second career following work in high-tech startups. He began as a hospital chaplain, focusing on mental health, and then became a parish minister, serving in Youngstown, Ohio, for eight years. He now serves as minister of the Lake Chapala Unitarian Universalist Fellowship in Ajijic, Jalisco, Mexico, where he enjoys hiking, reading, music, and exploring the area.

Barry Andrews, a retired Unitarian Universalist minister, has preached the gospel of Transcendentalism in Unitarian Universalist congregations on both coasts and in between. He's taught courses and written books about Transcendentalist spirituality and the major figures of the Transcendentalist movement: Ralph Waldo Emerson, Henry David Thoreau, and Margaret Fuller. His latest book is *Transcendentalism and the Cultivation of the Soul*, published by the University of Massachusetts Press.

Wayne B. Arnason retired from full-time ministry after a forty-year career of service to Unitarian Universalist congregations and institutions. He started a meditation practice in college and at the age of forty-five committed himself to a Soto Zen Buddhist practice with a teacher. He continues to sit within the Boundless Way Zen Community and to do a daily Tai Chi practice.

Laurie Bushbaum has been a Unitarian Universalist parish minister and minister of religious education since 1984. A semi-professional fiber artist, she loves making stuff out of old doilies, her grandmother's gloves, and fabric scraps traded among friends. In her last ministry setting, she made jewelry out of the old church silverware. She and her husband have a fairy garden for the neighborhood children, and she is convinced there is beauty everywhere!

Cynthia Cain lives on a farm in Kentucky where she is completing a collaborative photographic/written/recorded history of the nearby Black community, whose members are descendants of slaves owned by the ancestors of the white townsfolk. She holds an MFA in fiction and is a certified spiritual director. Now in her sixties, she is raising a fourth child, a great nephew with autism. She loves meditation, yoga, and travel.

Dawn Skjei Cooley is a Unitarian Universalist minister based in Louisville, Kentucky. When she and her family settled in Louisville, she realized she needed to make some non-church friends and also wanted to pick up a fun hobby. After watching the movie "Whip It," she knew that roller derby would meet both needs perfectly. She briefly played competitive roller derby as "LivFearless" with the Derby City Roller Girls.

Leia Durland-Jones, a lifelong Unitarian Universalist, serves as director of faith development at the Thomas Jefferson Memorial Church in Charlottesville, Virginia. She lives in Charlottesville with her wife and daughter. When traveling, she uses the Worldwide Labyrinth locator to experience labyrinths in the area. While on a pilgrimage with Judith Tripp in 2009, she was introduced to the Women's Dream Quest, a labyrinth-centered retreat held around the globe (including, now, Charlottesville!).

James Ishmael Ford is retired from Unitarian Universalist parish ministry after serving congregations for twenty-five years. He is currently a community minister affiliated with the Unitarian Universalist Church of Long Beach. He is also an ordained Zen Buddhist priest, a guiding teacher with the Boundless Way Zen Network, and resident teacher of the Blue Cliff Zen Sangha. His most recent book is *If You're Lucky, Your Heart Will Break: Field Notes from a Zen Life.*

Jon Cleland Host is a naturalistic pagan, scientist, father, science educator, and Unitarian Universalist. He has written religious education lessons and stories, contributed to the *Faith of UU Pagans* pamphlet, and contributed to the UU Common Ground pamphlet, among other writings. Outside of Unitarian Universalism, his spiritual work has included science outreach, blogging at Naturalpagans.com, and contributing to the book *Godless Paganism.*

Jonalu Johnstone has served as a Unitarian Universalist minister for more than twenty years. She has traveled a seeker's path, influenced by Christianity, Paganism, Taoism, and Buddhism. She's been a spiritual director since 2010 and currently serves the Unitarian Universalist Fellowship of Manhattan, Kansas, as developmental minister. She lives with her partner of more than thirty years, Jane Powell, a retired social worker and long-distance backpacker.

Jessica Lin lives in North Carolina and is a member of the Unitarian Universalist Fellowship of Raleigh. She loves to read, fly kites in the park, eat cheese, and plan themed parties, not usually all at the same time.

Sue Magidson is a Jewish Unitarian Universalist minister who delights in spiritual practices—journaling, meditation, prayer, painting, singing, taking long walks in nature, stopping to smell the roses or really look at a tree. Perhaps her favorite spiritual practice is serving as a hospital chaplain, where she endeavors to listen deeply for what is needed in each moment and to respond with love and compassion.

Susan Manker (aka Susan Manker-Seale) is a writer and Unitarian Universalist minister who has served congregations in California and Arizona. Her writings and poetry have been included in a variety of anthologies. She has been a board member of UU Mystics in Community for more than a decade, helping to lift up awareness of mystical experiences in Unitarian Universalism and their influence on spiritual practice.

Colleen McDonald resumed her piano practice in adulthood, when she and her husband, Jerry, were raising two daughters (adopted from the foster care system), and she was serving as minister of religious education at the Unitarian Universalist Church, Rockford, Illinois. She now has three grandchildren and works as an occupational therapist, working with special education students in the Rockford schools. She dedicates her essay in this book to her wise and patient piano teacher, Patricia Jeske.

Amy Zucker Morgenstern serves as minister to the Unitarian Universalist Church of Palo Alto. She strives daily to keep the commitment she and the congregation urge upon themselves at the closing benediction, to "speak love with word and deed," and fails frequently. She tries to live with passion, especially in making a good marriage with Joy Morgenstern and raising their daughter, Indigo. She is sustained by another imperative of the benediction that comes more easily: "Rejoice in beauty."

Linnea Nelson has found both joy and solace exploring spiritual practices as the director of religious exploration at the Unitarian Universalist Congregation of Fairfax and as a part of two Wellspring groups. She has experienced immense gratitude for everyday moments and a heightened appreciation for the people in her life, especially those in her lively household: Ted, a patient and wise spouse; Joel, a filmmaker and loyal friend; and Nick an adventurer and entrepreneur.

Ann Richards, a fifth-generation Unitarian Universalist, finds joy in her work as the director of lifespan spiritual growth at Mt. Vernon Unitarian Church in Alexandria, Virginia. She also finds joy in her friends from the Liberal Religious Educators Association, teaching knitting, movies, reading, and her family.

Jaelynn P. Scott lives in Washington State, where she spends her time among the great trees of the Pacific Northwest, wishing she could make a living roaming the forests. She is a Buddhist minister, ordained by the International Order of Buddhist Ministers, but doesn't take that too seriously. Her Buddhist practice looks pretty similar to that of Edina from the British sitcom *Absolutely Fabulous*: a few chimes of the gong, some chants, and then debauchery to follow. She and her ten-pound companion, Bodhi, have been in ministry together since 2015.

Aaron M. Stockwell has served as the developmental minister at the Unitarian Universalist Church of the Brazos Valley in College Station, Texas, since 2015. His two favorite seminary classes at Andover Newton Theological School were Pastoral Uses of Social Media and Spiritual Practices for Healing and Wholeness, which merged two deep interests of his: technology and spiritual practices. He has probably already taken a picture of this book and put it up on Instagram, with the perfect filter.

Arvid Straube served as a Unitarian Universalist parish minister for more than thirty years. He now works as a meditation coach, spiritual director, and seminary teacher. His own practice is grounded in the Vipassana (Insight) tradition of Buddhism and the Christian contemplative tradition. He loves travel, cooking, and deep conversations with wise friends. He lives near San Diego with his wife, Sonya Prestridge.

Erik Walker Wikstrom is a husband and father of two sons, neither of whom shows any interest in his father's hobbies. Prior to being ordained as a Unitarian Universalist minister, he was a juggler, magician, escape artist, clown, and fire eater. He is the author of three books and has been included in two anthologies—all published by Skinner House Books.